Angels
and
TRANSLATED BEINGS

By Howard Carlos Smith

Preface

Life after death. Angels are children of God. An angel may be a resurrected being, translated being, disembodied spirit, unembodied spirit, or a mortal such as you or I being attentive to the spirit of God.

Acknowledgment

My love is sent, by the way of prayer, to my mother Verla for instilling within me the desire to attend church and read good books as well as the value of daily prayer.

I express my love to my sweetheart and best friend Jolene for without her efforts and suggestions the book would not have come to be. She is the co-author of this book and is registered as such.

Special thanks to my cousin Lamar Noble and his wife Teri, for their friendship and willingness in sharing the sacred relics with the world.

Thanks to Blip Color for their hard work in printing this book. Thanks to Lorin Robbins for the book cover design.

And finally thanks to Brigham Distributing for distributing and placing into e-Book format this book as well as the two preceding books.

Howard Carlos Smith

Table of Contents

Pushed by an Angel

INTRODUCTION

My life has been one of much interest – mainly to myself. I was named Howard after Howard Hellewell my step-grandfather. Grandfather Hellewell delivered me as my mother was unable to make it to the hospital. My father, Kenneth, was on a work assignment in southern Utah. I am the last of four children, Colette, Dixie and Sondra. Dixie passed over as an infant and Sondra passed over several years ago.

At the age of four my father moved the family from Farmington ten miles south into the township of West Bountiful; a small community of small farms and old houses, just a hop-skip-and jump away from Salt Lake City. Our new two story home was of red brick situated on an acre of ground with a garage and large stable. A flowing artesian well was a bonus. Fresh ice cold mineral water flowed from an underground lake. Over a ditch of water from a mountain creek and across a dirt road was my uncle and aunt, Delbert and Bernice Noble's house and a thirty acre farm. Just a rock throw from their house was an old adobe house built by pioneer Joseph

Bates Noble. The home to which the 'Nauvoo Legion Sword' of the Prophet Joseph Smith was hid away. The story regarding this sword is covered in my first book *Keeper of the Prophet's Sword – Joseph Bates Noble Body Guard to the Prophet Joseph Smith*.

One winter day dad decided to take the family on a drive to visit friends in Farmington. It turned out to be a bad decision. He was driving a 1945 Chevrolet four door sedan with cork snow tires. Sondra, age 9, and I, age 7, were seated on the back seat. My parents and grandmother, Nancy Ellen Higley Hellewell, were the occupants of the front seat.

Nearing the Lagoon Resort a blanket of fog off the Great Salt Lake soon encircled our car. Dad realizing the dangerous conditions decided to turn the car about and point toward home. Shortly thereafter an angel spoke to me telling me to move quickly to the other side of the seat. I didn't react to the command so the angel without hesitation pushed me and Sondra quickly behind Dad at the steering wheel. I need to emphasis this was a very quick push. Seat belts were unheard of at that time.

I remember the noise as a huge fully loaded semi-truck came through the fog ramming into the rear of the car ripping off the section of seat where Sondra and I were previously seated. I was knocked unconscious and sustained a cracked skull and concussion. Sondra's arm was broken and she lost several of her front teeth. Grandma Hellewell received a broken leg. Mom and dad escaped injury. The angels' push saved me and Sondra from being crushed and killed.

I was unconscious for two days with mother attending to me as I slept upon a make shift bed in the living room. I have a faint memory of being in another world during my black-out time. After awakening I remember having an extreme headache and the family was all around me. There was a lot of homemade ice cream and a wake-up call every hour.

A Walk Together – Jedediah & Bates

CHAPTER 1

Bates and Jedediah crossed paths in Kirtland, Ohio, quickly became close friends and were almost like brothers. Joseph Bates Noble was born June 14, 1810 in Egremont, Massachusetts. He was baptized in 1832 by Brigham Young. Jedediah Morgan Grant was born on February 21, 1816. Both attended Zion's Camp.

In February 1834 the Lord revealed to Joseph Smith, the Mormon Prophet, that he should organize an army of men to march one thousand miles from Kirtland, Ohio into Missouri and help restore the Saints into their lands. Their homes, barns, haystacks and farms were being burned to the ground by the mobs. Like an older brother Bates walked along side Jedediah on the trek. Bates was age 24 and Jedediah was age 18.

Along the way across Indiana the two soldiers witnessed Martin Harris offer his naked toe to a five foot black snake. It was sunning in the middle of a dirt road. When the snake refused to bite, Martin proclaimed an apostolic victory. Later he repeated the experiment with another snake of similar length receiving a severe bite on the ankle. [1]

Crossing Illinois and into Missouri, Joseph Smith shared many stories regarding the Lamanite and Nephite nations that once harbored this land of America.

Joseph Bates Noble remarked in his journal, "I have somewhere among my papers a brief sketch of places, distances and things that transpired on the way."[2] These sketches are missing from his journal. Hopefully in the future it will come forth, perhaps someone in the Noble family has possession of them.

Jedediah and Bates served as members of the First Quorum of Seventy, each attended the School of the Prophets and were taught many things including Hebrew. Each served as body guards to

JOSEPH SMITH, JR. ZIONS CAMP MARCH 1834

We arrived this morning on the banks of the Mississippi ...we left the eastern part of the state of Ohio...The whole of our journey, in the midst of so large a company of social honest and sincere men, wandering over the mounds of that once beloved people of the Lord, picking up their skulls & bones, as proud of its divine authenticity and gazing upon the country the fertility, the splendor and the goodness so indescribable ...Joseph Smith, Jr. (Letter to Emma Smith, June 4, 1834), Dean C. Jesse, *"The Personal Writings of Joseph Smith,"* page 324. Salt Lake City, Utah. Deseret Book Co. 1984.

Also Ancient American Archaeology – Special LDS Edition IV, by Wayne N. May. ancientamerican.com

---

[1] 'No Man Knows My History', by Fawn M. Brodie, 2nd Edition, 1962, p. 147
[2] Journal of Joseph Bates Noble, Noble Family History, p. 3

Joseph Smith and were officers in the Nauvoo Legion. At times both families shared dinner at Emma and Joseph's house as if they were one large family.

Moving ahead to the Salt Lake valley, Jedediah would marry Susan Noble, the youngest sister of Joseph Bates Noble. Susan was 15 years old when she walked the plains to the Salt Lake Valley. Her brother Bates led a pioneer company of 171 and Jedediah with his company of 150 entered the Salt Lake Valley back-to-back in late September and early October 1847.[3]

Crossing the plains was difficult for all who came as entire families. Many saints were not able to bear the arduous journey dying on the way. While at Winter Quarters Joseph Bates Noble's wife Sarah became extremely ill and crossed over in the arms of her husband. It was a short life at age twenty-seven. Jedediah Morgan Grant was there to assist his friend.

Jedediah, captain of the 3rd Company, lost his wife Caroline and their infant daughter Margaret, who like many others, contracted cholera on the Sweetwater River. Caroline died four days after her daughter. Before her death, she requested that their bodies be buried in the valley, but Jedediah was forced to inter the baby in a shallow grave and continue on to the Salt Lake Valley where he buried his wife. Then he and his friend Joseph Bates Noble returned to the Wyoming plains to exhume Margaret's body, only to find that wolves had found the grave first.

---

[3] Church History Chapters 26-30. Also
http://www.ldsces.org/inst_manuals/chft/chft-26-30.htm

But before they reached the grave, the spirit of God had already comforted him. Jedediah confided to his friend, "Bates, God has made it plain. The joy of Paradise where my wife and baby are together, seems to be upon me tonight. For some wise purpose they have been released from the earth struggles into which you and I are plunged. They are many, many times happier than we can possibly be here." They returned to Salt Lake.[4]

Several years later Jedediah was permitted to see his wife and daughter in the world of spirits. Not long before Jedediah died, Heber C. Kimball gave him a blessing. On that occasion Jedediah related a vision he had received. "He saw the righteous gathered together in the spirit world, and there were no wicked spirits among them. He saw his wife; she was the first person that came to him. He saw many that he knew, but did not have conversation with any except his wife Caroline. She came to him, and he said that she looked beautiful and had their little child, that died on the plains, in her arms, and said, 'Mr. Grant, here is little Margaret; you know that the wolves ate her up, but it did not hurt her; see she is all right.'"[5]

Bates married Sylvia Loretta Mecham in January, 1857. Loretta shared in building a new brick adobe house in West Bountiful, Utah which sheltered the large family of eleven children. Hidden away in an upper bedroom was a casket cane and Joseph Smith's Nauvoo Legion sword. Downstairs on a corner table and within the family Bible

---

[4] http://www.ldsces.org/inst_manuals/chft/chft-26-30.htm
[5] Remarks at the Funeral of President Jedediah M. Grant by President Heber C. Kimball, Made in the Tabernacle, Great Salt Lake City, December 4, 1856. Reported by J. V. Long – 'Journal of Discourses'.

were the hair locks of Joseph and Hyrum Smith. The adobe house stood for one hundred years (1857 – 1957).

Following the instructions of the prophet, the Legion sword was passed from father to son for three generations of time into our day. It is no accident that my first cousin Lamar Noble has the sword that was hidden away for one hundred sixty-five years in West Bountiful, Utah. The spirit touched Lamar and I was asked to be the 'protector of the Legion sword', to share it with the world as directed by an angel – Joseph Bates Noble.

After 174 years and by permission, the Legion sword and casket stick were mounted securely in a walnut glass case and unveiled for the world to see at a Book of Mormon conference held at the Zermatt Resort in Midway, Utah October 2009. It was shared by way of two television stations at three different times and in many newspapers.[6]

Heber C. Kimball shares a conversation with Jedediah shortly before his passing. "Before brother Grant was taken sick, he said that he had unsheathed his sword, and that it never should be sheathed again until the enemies of righteousness were subdued; and he fought the devil up to the last, that he should not prevail on this earth. I can say that he left us with his sword unsheathed, and he will help Joseph and Hyrum and Willard.

"He said to me, 'Brother Heber, I have been into the spirit world two nights in succession, and, of all of the dreads that ever came across me, the worst was to have to again

---

[6] www.KeeperOfTheProphetsSword.com/gallery YouTube "Joseph Smith's Lieutenant Generals Sword Unveiling Oct. 2, 2009"

return to my body, though I had to do it. But O,' says he, 'the order and government that were there! When in the spirit world, I saw the order of righteous men and women; beheld them organized in their several grades, and there appeared to be no obstruction to my vision; I could see every man and woman in their grade and order. I looked to see whether there was any disorder there, but there was none; neither could I see any death nor any darkness, disorder or confusion.' He said that the people he there saw were organized in family capacities; and when he looked at them he saw grade after grade, and all were organized and in perfect harmony. He would mention one item after another and say, 'Why, it is just as brother Brigham says it is; it is just as he has told us many a time'.

"'Some may marvel at my speaking about these things, for many profess to believe that we have no spiritual existence. But do you not believe that my spirit was organized before it came to my body here? And do you not think there can be houses and gardens, fruit trees, and every other good thing there? The spirits of those things were made, as well as our spirits, and it follows that they can exist upon the same principle.

"'I saw flowers of numerous kinds, and some with from fifty to a hundred different colored flowers growing upon one stalk.' We have many kinds of flowers on the earth, and I suppose those very articles came from heaven, or they would not be here.

"After mentioning the things that he had seen, he spoke of how much he disliked to return and resume his body, after having seen the beauty and glory of the spirit world, where the righteous spirits are gathered there.

"'To my astonishment,' he said, 'when I looked at families there was a deficiency in some, there was a lack, for I saw families that would not be permitted to come and dwell together, because they had not honored their calling here.'

'He asked his wife Caroline where Joseph and Hyrum and Father Smith and others were; she replied, 'They have gone away ahead, to perform and transact business for us. The same as when Brother Brigham and his brethren left Winter Quarters and came here to search out a home; they came to find a location for their brethren'.

"He also spoke of the buildings he saw there, remarking that the Lord gave Solomon wisdom and poured gold and silver into his hands that he might display his skill and ability, and said that the temple erected by Solomon was much inferior to the most ordinary buildings he saw in the spirit world.

"After speaking of the gardens and the beauty of everything there, Brother Grant said that he felt extremely sorrowful at having to leave so beautiful a place and come back to earth, for he looked upon his body with loathing, but was obliged to enter it again.

"He said that after he came back he could look upon his family and see the spirit that was in them, and the darkness that was in them; and that he conversed with them about the Gospel, and what they should do, and they replied, 'Well, brother Grant, perhaps it is so, and perhaps it is not,' and said that was the state of this people, to a great extent, for many are full of darkness and will not believe me.

"I never had a view of the righteous assembling in the spirit world, but I have had a view of the hosts of hell, and have seen them as plainly as I see you today. The righteous spirits gather together to prepare and qualify themselves for a future day, and evil spirits have no power over them, though they are constantly striving for the mastery. I have seen evil spirits attempt to overcome those holding the Priesthood and I know how they act."[7]

---

[7] Remarks at the Funeral of President Jedediah M. Grant by President Heber C. Kimball, Made in the Tabernacle, Great Salt Lake City, December 4, 1856. Reported by J. V. Long – Journal of Discourses.

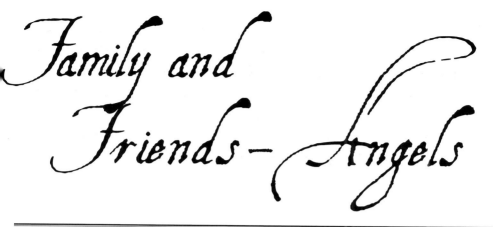

CHAPTER 2

The Lord explains to Joseph Smith . . . "That which is spiritual being in the likeness of that which is temporal; and that which is temporal in the likeness of that which is spiritual; the spirit of man in the likeness of his person, as also the spirits of the beast, and every other creature which God has created."[1]

Angels are people in form; they have faces, eyes, ears, torsos, arms, hands and feet. They see each other, hear each other, and talk with each other. In short, nothing proper to man whatsoever is missing except that angels are not clothed with a dirt body.[2]

The 'Origin of Man' as declared by the Church states, "'God created man in His own image.'[3] This is just as true of the spirit as it is of the body, which is only the clothing of the spirit, it complements the two together constituting the soul. The spirit of man is in the form of man, and the

[1] D & C 77:2
[2] 'Heaven and Hell', pp. 70-71
[3] Improvement Era, November 1909, p. 77

spirits of all creatures are in the likeness of their bodies."[4]

We too after death may become angels visiting our love ones by permission in times of need. A time when our soul is longing and reaching out for comfort, a mother, father, son, daughter or grandparents who have departed may visit. Angel visits are normal to me, it's been that way since I was a lad working on the farm.

Melvin J. Ballard wrote of himself: "I lost a son six years of age, and I saw him a man in the spirit world after his death, and I saw how he had exercised his own freedom of choice and would obtain of his own will and volition of companionship in due time to him and all those who are worthy of it, shall come all of the blessings and sealing privileges of the House of the Lord."[5]

Marriner W. Merrill relates a visit with his son: "On one occasion soon after the death of his son, as he was returning to his home, he was in his carriage so deeply lost in thought about his son that he was quite oblivious to things about him. He suddenly came into a state of awareness when his horse stopped in the road. As he looked up, his son stood in the road beside him. His son spoke to him and said, 'Father, you are mourning my departure unduly. You are over concerned about my family (his son left a large family of small children) and their welfare. I have much work to do and your grieving gives me much concern. I am in a position to render effective service to my family. You should take comfort,

---

[4] This First Presidency statement is also in the Encyclopedia of Mormonism, 4:1665-69.
[5] 'Three Degrees of Glory', p. 31. Also 'Faith Precedes the Miracle', p. 335.

for you know there is much work to be done here and it was necessary for me to be called. You know that the Lord doeth all things well.' So saying, the son departed."[6]

Joseph Smith said, "The Lord takes many away even in infancy, that they may escape the envy of man and the sorrows and evils of this present world; they were too pure, too lovely, to live on this earth. Therefore, if rightly considered, instead of mourning we have reason to rejoice as they are delivered from evil and we shall have them again. The only difference between the old and the young dying is, one lives longer in heaven and eternal light and glory than the other, and is freed a little sooner from this miserable world."[7]

Spencer W. Kimball shares an extension of life given to his uncle David Patten Kimball about November, 1881. 'My uncle, David Patten Kimball, left his home in Arizona on a trip across the Salt River desert. He had fixed up his books and settled accounts and had told his wife of a premonition that he would not return. He was lost on the desert for two days and three nights, suffering untold agonies of thirst and pain. He passed into the spirit world and described later, in a letter of January 8, 1882, to his sister, what happened there. He had seen his parents. "My father . . . told me I could remain there if I chose to do so, but I pled with him that I might stay with my family long enough to make them comfortable, to repent of my sins, and more fully prepare myself for the change. Had it not been for this, I never should have returned home, except as a corpse. Father finally told me I could

---

[6] Bryant S. Hinckley, 'The Faith of Our Pioneer Fathers', pp. 182-183.
[7] 'Faith Precedes the Miracle', Discourses of Spencer W. Kimball, 1977, p. 103.

remain two years and to do all the good I could during this time, after which he would come for me . . . He mentioned four others that he would come for also . . . Two years to the day from that experience on the desert he died easily and apparently without pain. Shortly before he died he looked up and called, "Father, Father." Within approximately a year of his death the other four men named were also dead.'[8]

As mortals we are spiritual beings inhabiting human bodies; when empowered by the Lord to do so, our spirits are able to leave our bodies at death, or at other times such as an out-of-body experience when we leave and then return.

Your spirit body will be perfect again. For example, a quadriplegic is no longer paralyzed, multiple sclerosis patients who have been in wheelchairs for years say that when they are out of their body they can sing and dance.

Guy Pierce, a good friend of mine and fellow shop teacher at Hillcrest High School in Midvale, Utah, experienced a life changing accident and overnight became a quadriplegic. He raced dirt bikes (motorcycles). One day as he was racing the bike flipped over and injured his spinal column. It was a tough situation yet Guy came out on top completing a Master's Degree and was a few hours short of receiving his Doctorate Degree at the University of Utah. Although he couldn't feed himself he became very skilled in operating his motorized wheelchair. With the touch of a finger Guy could zip his chair through a door opening missing the sides narrowly. He was my hero, he always had a smile, was positive in his speech

---

[8] Ibid, pp. 104-105.

and there to help you in anyway. I'm a better person today because of this dear friend.

Shortly after running for Circuit Judge, Guy crossed over. I was unaware of his death. One morning around 4 A.M. I had a visit from him by vision or dream yet it was real. Guy appeared to me sitting in his wheelchair, a smile on his face and glowing like an angel. Before his accident he stood around 6'1" and over 200 pounds. He appeared healthy and tall. He suddenly jumped out of his wheelchair walked over to me and gave me a brotherly hug. My wife picked up a newspaper that morning and in the obituary section was a picture of Guy and an announcement of the funeral. We contacted his wife and attended the celebration of his life. The seats were overflowing with students who once attended his wood working class. Guy was truly a craftsman and shared his talents.

Take the Spirit from the Body

CHAPTER 3

"Take the spirit from the body," Brigham Young declared, "and the body is lifeless."[1]

Once the spirit escapes your mortal body, the body is dead. One looks upon his or her body as three dimensional to which a mirror does not reflect. One soon realizes the body is not real to them but only a house they lived in while in the earth – it is easy to understand why they no longer feel any strong attachment to it. The spirit seems to grasp the purpose of the earthly body as a temple or house for a divine, immortal spirit. The spirit never dies, it's never ending, surely it looks forward to the resurrection a time of the renewed body, a body that does not wear out.

At times those who have lost a friend or loved one often have a sensation when viewing a body of the deceased that it no longer closely resembles the living person who was known. One may ask, what is missing?

---

[1] 'Journal of Discources', 9:287

Joseph Smith declared, "There is no such thing as immaterial matter. All spirit is matter, but it is more fine or pure, and can only be discerned by purer eyes; we cannot see it; but when our bodies are purified we shall see that it is all matter."[2]

An account was published in 1889 in the St. Louis Medical and Surgical Journal by Dr. A. Wiltse who 'died' of typhoid fever and returned. He detailed his spirit leaving his body and said, "As I turned, my left elbow came in contact with an arm of one gentleman, who was standing at my door. To my surprise, his arm passed through mine without apparent resistance, the severed parts closing again without pain, as air reunites."[3]

Charles W. Penrose spoke regarding spirit substance; "A spiritual person can take the hand of another spiritual person and it is substantial. A person in the body could not grasp a spirit, for that spirit has different properties to those of our bodies and it is governed by different laws to those that govern us in this sphere of mortality. A spiritual substance, organized into form, occupies room and space just as much in its sphere as these natural particles occupy in this sphere."[4]

When someone has an out of body experience and actually visits the spirit world it's the spirit that arrives, the mortal body will stay where it is. That's hard to comprehend yet while visiting you can embrace your father, mother, grandparents or others upon your arrival. It is no different than embracing others in your mortal body.

---

[2] D & C 131:7-8
[3] As quoted in 'Life at Death', p. 230
[4] Journal of Discourses, 26:22

People in the spirit world are not all in white clothing, they dress as we do; sometimes on a special assignment they may appear in pure white which is above the luster of the sun or in cream colored robes. It is my opinion that their robes are temple clothing. My mother has visited me several times once in a cream robe and other times in her best dress as she would wear to church meetings. The clothing is very fancy, colorful and pleasing to the eye. After her death she visited several of her grandchildren wearing a cream robe. My cousin June Noble visited me shortly after her passing wearing a white robe with a glow about her body and a whiteness beyond earthly description.

In the world of spirits we still have our free agency as directed by God. Each person, someday in the future, will be resurrected, assigned to a planet adapted to their faithfulness in keeping God's commandments. People there do not dress according to intelligence, they dress according to their work and desires. They may be farmers, going to school, on missions, or other endeavors. Church attendance continues in that realm however on a higher degree and there is temple work along with assignments to this earth assisting at assisted living homes, hospitals, etc. It is a very busy place with no idleness. Some may be guardian angels to family members in this life.

When I saw my mother in the spirit world she was working in a flower shop in a busy part of town. She had flowers of many colors and the colors were indescribable when compared to flowers in mortal life. She wore a dress of many colors, she was young with long auburn hair and very happy with a brightness that seemed to radiate about her spirit.

What about communicating spirit to spirit from a visiting angel? My experience reveals a thought process, a pure language yet very natural.

Patriarch Eldred G. Smith provided an analogy regarding spiritual communication. He said, "Now, I think if we will apply some of the laws of electronics, that is, radio and television, we will be aided in a possible understanding of how we can receive a message from the Holy Ghost. We have a spirit mind and a mortal mind. Our spirit mind can receive messages from the Holy Ghost, who is a spirit. In this room now there are many waves going by of sound, of pictures, and even of colored pictures. We cannot detect them with our mortal eyes or ears, but if we set up a receiving set and put it in tune, then we pick up the sound or pictures by the mortal ears or eyes. Similarly, the Holy Ghost may be constantly sending out messages like a broadcasting station. If you put yourself in tune, that is, knock or ask or seek, you may receive the message. It may be as if you were to open an imaginary window or door between your spirit mind and your physical mind and permit the message to come through. Spirit can talk to spirit, and you are part spirit – just open that imaginary door and let the mortal mind receive."[5]

Whether in the body or out we are people with grandparents going back to Adam and Eve. In the spirit world or this world we are literally brothers and sisters. Angels talk with each other just the way people in this

---

[5] Elder Eldred G. Smith, Conference Report, October 1964, pp. 10-11

world do, they talk about various things - political matters, household, recreation, church, etc.

Soon all will be in the next life. Earth life is very short and the passage of time is like a dream – it comes and goes. There we will remember everything we have learned and done in this life.

George Q. Cannon said: "Memory will be quickened to a wonderful extent. Every deed that we have done will be brought to our recollection. Every acquaintance made will be remembered. There will be no scenes or incidents in our lives that will be forgotten by us in the world to come. You have heard of men who have been drowning or have fallen from a great height describe that in about a second or two every event of their lives passed before them like a panorama with the rapidity of lightning. This shows what power there is latent to the human mind, which, when quickened by the power of God, will make men and women recall not only that which pertains to this life, but our memories will stretch back to the life we had before we came here, with the associations we had with our Father and God and with those bright spirits that stand around His throne and with the righteous and holy ones."[6]

Heber E. Hale experienced an out of body experience and left this testimony, "The people I met there, did not think of themselves as spirit but as men and women, self-thinking, and self-acting individuals, going about important business in a most orderly manner. There was

---

[6] 'Gospel Truth', pp. 60-61

perfect order there, and everybody had something to do and seemed to be about their business." [7]

Joseph F. Smith believed we are watched over and guided here by those who cared to us while they were in the earth. He said, "I believe we move and have our being in the presence of heavenly messengers and of heavenly beings. We are not separate from them. We begin to realize more and more fully, as we become acquainted with the principles of the Gospel, as they have been revealed anew in this dispensation, that we are closely related to our kindred, to our ancestors, to our friends and associates and co-laborers who have preceded us into the spirit world. . . . And therefore, I claim that we live in their presence, they see us, they are solicitous of our welfare, and they love us now more than ever. For now they see the dangers that beset us; they can comprehend better than ever before, the weaknesses that are liable to mislead us into dark and forbidden paths. They see the temptations and the evils that beset us in life and the proneness of mortal beings to yield to temptation and to wrong doing; hence their solicitude for us and their love for us and their desire for our well-being must be greater than that which we feel for ourselves." [8]

---

[7] As quoted in 'Life Everlasting', p. 79
[8] As quoted in 'The Life Beyond', pp. 83-84

Paradise is Not Heaven

CHAPTER 4

Paradise is not heaven or the place where God dwells but a place of departed spirits. From the time Jesus Christ's spirit left his body until he arose from the tomb he was with the thief and others in paradise, according to His promise. There the Savior opened the door for the salvation of the dead. Before that time the unworthy dead were shut up in prison and were not visited.[1]

A partial judgment takes place at separation when the spirit being departs this mortal body. The mortal body now dead decays, soon returning as dirt and back into mother earth. The spirit being moves on into the spirit world. Some spirits enter paradise while others enter the spirit prison. It is prison in the sense that the spirit is not yet ready for a higher level of paradise living among the prophets of God and beings who lived the commandments while in the earth.

Joseph F. Smith in his vision of the dead said, "I beheld that the faithful elders of this dispensation, when they depart from mortal life, continue their labors in preaching

---

[1] Pearl of Great Price, Moses 7:38-39; Isaiah 24:22

of the Gospel of repentance and redemption, through the sacrifice of the Only Begotten Son of God, among those who are in darkness and under the bondage of sin in the great world of the spirits of the dead."[2]

As we know Jesus Christ and Michael, under the direction of God the Father, are the makers of this home we call earth. There are three levels to this earth. After being instructed by an angel Corianton recorded thus: "Now, concerning the state of the soul between death and the resurrection – Behold, it has been made known unto me by an angel, that the spirits of all men, as soon as they are departed from this mortal body, yea the spirits of all men, whether they be good or evil, are taken home to that God who gave them life."[3]

We will go to paradise, spirit prison, or to hell with Satan, waiting and working towards our day of resurrection. Those who go to hell, under the earth, are there for the duration until the last resurrection. This allows the wicked spirits time to think things over as to their deeds done in the earth.

Corianton continues, "And then it shall come to pass, that the spirits of the wicked, yea, who are evil – for behold, they have no part nor portion of the Spirit of the Lord; for behold, they chose evil works rather than good, therefore the spirit of the devil did enter into them, and take possession of their house – and these shall be cast out into outer darkness; there shall be weeping, and

---

[2] Gospel Doctrine, p. 601
[3] Alma 40:11

29

wailing, and gnashing of teeth, and this because of their own iniquity, being led captive by the will of the devil."[4]

If these evil beings have crossed your path in this life causing havoc to your family, etc. upon separation you will go into the world of spirits and the evil ones will go down under the earth into Hell. More than likely you'll never cross paths with them again.

Corianton continues, "Now this is the state of the souls of the wicked, yea, in darkness, and a state of awful, fearful looking for the fiery indignation of the wrath of God upon them; thus they remain in this state, as well as the righteous in paradise, until the time of their resurrection."[5]

"And then shall it come to pass, that the spirits of those who are righteous are received into a state of happiness, which is called paradise, a state of rest, a state of peace, where they shall rest from all their troubles and for all care and sorrow."[6]

The angel stated it as it is. After this mortal stage of partial judgment we go to paradise, spirit prison or hell. All of these are separate places, yet missionaries can cross over into the spirit prison and back into paradise.

The spirit world is a wonderful place to live, especially paradise. Just think...you are now young, no sickness, no death, no bad weather, no clouds. There is a bright blue sky, an orange yellow sun providing a radiating warmth at the perfect temperature, perhaps a slight breeze flowing in and around your spirit body providing

---

4 Alma 40:13
5 Alma 40:14
6 Alma 40:12

additional comfort. No pollution of any kind, there are no cars, airplanes, freeways, light poles, or wind generators; nevertheless there are cities throughout the spirit world some with the same names as our section of earth. Even in the prison area the spirit beings are much happier than when they were experiencing mortal life.

It is a 'heaven' in which men and women prepare their lives always looking forward to their resurrection day; anticipating a new home on another planet (Terrestrial) or a renewed (Celestial) earth. A reward for the faithfulness in earth and progression in the world of spirits. Each a heaven and reward for good deeds.

The preaching of this Gospel is now going on with full power among the spirits; while we here in the earth as faithful saints with oil in our lamps are laboring industriously in the temples of the Lord to give to our kindred dead the opportunity to receive blessings and ordinances required for their salvation.

Missionary work is not just for the elders. Joseph Fielding Smith shared his knowledge of the missionary work being moved along by women in a talk at a funeral celebration for Mary A. Freeze. "Now, among all these millions of spirits that have lived on the earth and have passed away, from generation to generation, since the beginning of the world, without the knowledge of the Gospel – among them you may count that at least one-half are women. Who is going to preach the Gospel to the women? Who is going to carry the testimony of Jesus Christ to the hearts of the women who have passed away without a knowledge of the Gospel? Well, to my mind, it is a simple thing. These good sisters who have been set apart, ordained to the work, called to it, authorized by the authority of the Holy Priesthood to minister to their sex, in the House of God for the living and for the dead, will be fully authorized and empowered to preach the Gospel and minister to the women while the elders and prophets are preaching it to the men. The things we experience here are typical of the things of God, and the life beyond us."[7]

---

[7] Gospel Doctrine, pp. 581-582

Learning Continues as Spirits

CHAPTER 5

Learning continues beyond the grave. To cease growing and advancing would be a spiritual damnation. Brigham Young speaks as to moving on. "And then we shall go on from step to step, from rejoicing to rejoicing, and one in intelligence and power to another, our happiness becoming more and more exquisite and sensible as we proceed in the words and power in life."[1]

A story is told about a man being led by a spirit guide to a vast, old library containing the wisdom of the ages, everything ever said or written. ". . . My guide . . . told me I must study and learn from the infinite array of wisdom before us. I was dismayed, and said there was no way I was capable of such a task. I was told to simply make a beginning, to do the best I could, and that would always be good enough. There was plenty of time."[2]

As I look back over the years my thoughts center around an old high school buddy of whom I lost track. He never

---

[1] 'Journal of Discourses' 6:349
[2] 'Journal of Near-Death Studies', Vol. 10, No. 1, Fall 1991, p. 31

came to the school reunions and no one knew where he lived. Kent played football for Bountiful High School. My sport was wrestling. We each received our lettering jacket signifying our sport. Upon graduating Kent and I joined the Utah National Guard. We were separated into different units and sent to different locations in the country.

During a high school football game Kent was severely injured while making a tackle. This injury hindered him physically later on and for the rest of his life as he is unable to do physical work. During his army days the injury went unnoticed. Yet later it became more pronounced as he became hunched back unable to stand straight and while walking always having to look down rather than straight ahead.

One early morning hour I experienced a dream. It is just as vivid today as it was then. I found myself in the spirit world visiting a college campus. It was between classes, people with books in hand making their way to the next class. I was unnoticed yet I felt uneasy for all the students were vibrant and young in spirit. I felt like an aged man in their presence.

Soon I found myself at a hallway intersection where a group of students were standing and chatting. One young man caught my eye. It was my buddy Kent. In this group he was a towering spirit, taller than me, weighing well over two hundred pounds and very muscular. He looked to be in his early thirties. He was happy, had many friends and much into his schooling. We looked into each other's eyes. At first he did not recognize me. Yet as I walked toward him his memory of our friendship returned. We embraced shortly, had a nice chat and soon I was on my way.

Parley P. Pratt in speaking about the realm of the spirit world said, "It is an intermediate state, a probation, a place of preparation, improvement, instruction, education, where spirits are chastened, and improved and where, if found worthy; they may be taught a knowledge of the Gospel. In short, it is a place where the Gospel is preached, and where faith, repentance, hope, and charity may be exercised; a place of waiting for the resurrection or redemption of the body."[3]

Brigham Young stated, "I shall not cease learning while I live, nor when I arrive in the spirit world; but shall there learn with greater facility; and when I again receive my body, I shall learn a thousand times more in a thousand times less time; and then I do not mean to cease learning, but shall still continue my researches . . . We shall never see the time when we shall not need to be taught, nor when there will not be an object to be gained."[4]

---

[3] 'Key to the Science of Theology', p. 80
[4] 'Discourses of Brigham Young', by John A. Widtsoe, 1966, p. 248.

A Whispering in My Ear

CHAPTER 6

As a missionary for the Church of Jesus Christ of Latter-day Saints, my first assignment was in Miami, Florida. In those days the area was large; it included parts of Alabama, Georgia and all of Florida. Nearing the end of my mission President David O. McKay opened up the island of Puerto Rico and it became a part of my mission. Our Mission President, Ned Winder, received an early morning telephone call from the Prophet and shortly thereafter I received an early morning telephone call from President Winder. I was asked to pack my bags, catch a bus from Jacksonville to Miami, Florida and board a plane. I was one of three missionaries to open up the island for the preaching of the Gospel. This completed the last five months of a two year mission. It was a life changing event for me. Elder Weston Parker from Ovid, Idaho was my companion.

During my first assignment as a missionary, Elder Douglas Stroup was my first companion. We lived in an old motel room in Miami, Florida. Somehow the outgoing

Mission President paired up two "green" missionaries quite by accident. We had quite the experiences and someday there may be a book written about the 'two greenies' of Opa-Locka, Florida. Shortly after completing my mission the old Opa-Locka LDS chapel burned to the ground.

I would like to share a missionary experience I had with an angel. We had knocked on a door of the Blair Conner family, a family consisting of the parents, a daughter and a son. The Holy Ghost guided two greenie missionaries as we set up a time for a missionary discussion. It was a great success and shortly thereafter we baptized the entire family. The baptism was held at the Opa-Locka chapel on Saturday. The next day was Ward Conference. The Conner family attended and sat at the back of the chapel. Elder Stroup and I were seated near the front row. There was no one sitting to my right – the bench was empty yet the chapel was overflowing with people and the spirit was strong.

The Stake President was conducting the meeting. I was sitting very relaxed listening intently to the speaker when suddenly, without warning, a voice whispers into my right ear and states, "Elder Smith, you are going to be the next speaker." I look to my right and the bench is empty. Again, the voice whispers into my ear the same message as before. I look to my right and the bench is still empty. One more time the spirit whispers into my ear. I am in complete shock. I can hardly believe what just happened. I nudge Elder Stroup and tell him about the voice.

The speaker ends his talk and the Stake President stands to announce his next speaker. "At this time, though unusual, we would like to ask a fairly new missionary

Elder Smith from Bountiful, Utah to stand and share his testimony." I was shaking in my shoes. However the spirit was with me and I delivered a powerful testimony.

After my testimony the Stake President says, "I would like to invite a new member of the Church, Brother Blair Conner, who was just baptized last night with his wife and children to come up and share his testimony." Brother Conner walked up also shaking in his shoes (more so than me), stood erect at the pulpit and with the spirit of the Lord delivered a powerful testimony as to the truthfulness of the Gospel. It was Brother Conner's first time to share his testimony and his bottom lip was quivering. It was a beautiful testimony, the spirit bore witness to over three hundred saints in attendance.

I remember, as a lad, being told by my priesthood advisor that angels record our testimonies into a book in heaven. It is the Book of Life. Angels like to record all the good things we do, especially in helping others. We never know who is watching over us and protecting us from harm's way. Perhaps an angel also whispered in Brother Conner's ear . . . I never asked.

In December 1987, the Church Ensign magazine had a write up covering "The Many Faces of Miami Saints" by Editor Jim Gay. A color picture of Bishop Blair Conner is on page twenty. Editor Gay said, "In 1982 the Miami First Ward was dissolved and the building sold, Bishop Blair D. Conner formerly bishop of the First Ward, became bishop of the Hollywood Ward when the change was made."[1]

---

[1] Ensign, 'The Many Faces of Miami's Saints', by Jim Gay, December, 1987, pp. 18-22.

Later, a friend to Bishop Conner stated, "But for the Miami Saints it is not a matter merely of obedience; their love seems to flow naturally." Sister Davis explains, "You get to feeling so close to each other that when somebody is not there, you want to find out what happened."[2]

---

[2] Ibid, p. 22

Three Days with the Savior

CHAPTER 7

In our day one of my favorite apostles is Elder David B. Haight a man from Oakley, Idaho. A journey just eleven miles south of our house. As a lad David, more than likely bare footed, at times wandered over the foothills south of Oakley. At age 97 as an Apostle to the Lord Jesus Christ, Elder Haight passed over into the spirit world (1906-2004).

President Gordon B. Hinckley speaking at his funeral said, "He who lived longer than any apostle in this dispensation; when one is almost 98 years of age you know that the end can be imminent. But oh, how we shall miss him. How we will miss his sound judgment, his wise and convincing observations. How we will miss his quick humor, and most of all his stirring testimony.[1]

Elder Haight spoke at the 1989 General Conference of the Church. We listened intently to a very unusual talk. His voice is just as vivid today as it was that hour. During this talk he said, "One evening at home I experienced a

---

[1] Church News, published August 7, 2004.

health crisis; I knew something very serious was happening to me. It all happened so swiftly . . . the pain striking with such intensity. My dear Ruby phoning the doctor and me on my knees leaning over the bathtub for support and some comfort and hoped relief from the pain. I was pleading to my Heavenly Father to spare my life a while longer to give me more time to do His work; if it was His will. While still praying, I began to lose consciousness. The siren of the paramedic truck was the last I remember before unconsciousness overtook me.[2]"

Elder Haight went into a coma for three days; a time during which his spirit left his body and went off on a wonderful sojourn with the Lord and angels as his touring guides. "The terrible pain and commotion of people ceased. I was now in a calm, peaceful setting; all was serene and quiet. I was conscious of two persons in the distance on a hillside, one standing on a higher level than the other. Detailed features were not discernible. The person on the higher level was pointing to something I could not see.

"I heard no voices but was conscious of being in a holy presence and atmosphere. During the hours and days that followed, there was impressed again and again upon my mind the eternal mission and exalted position of the Son of Man. I witness to you that He is Jesus the Christ, the Son of God, Savior to all, Redeemer of all mankind, Bestower of infinite love, mercy, and forgiveness, the Light and Life of the world. I knew this truth before – I had never doubted nor wondered. But now I knew, because of the impressions of the Spirit upon my heart and soul, these divine truths in a most unusual way.

---

[2] Ibid.

"I was shown a panoramic view of His earthly ministry: His baptism, His teaching, His healing the sick and lame, the mock trial, His crucifixion, His resurrection and ascension. There followed scenes of His earthly ministry to my mind in impressive detail, confirming scriptural eyewitness accounts. I was being taught, and the eyes of my understanding were opened by the Holy Spirit of God so as to behold many things.

"The first scene was of the Savior and His Apostles in the upper chamber on the eve of His betrayal. Following the Passover supper, He instructed and prepared the sacrament of the Lord's Supper for His dearest friends as a remembrance of His coming sacrifice. It was so impressively portrayed to me – the overwhelming love of the Savior for each. I witnessed His thoughtful concern for significant details – the washing of the dusty feet of each Apostle, His breaking and blessing of the loaf of dark bread and blessing of the wine, then His dreadful disclosure that one would betray Him.

"When they had sung a hymn, Jesus and the Eleven went out to the Mount of Olives. There, in the garden, in some manner beyond our comprehension, the Savior took upon Himself the burden of the sins of mankind from Adam to the end of the world. His agony in the garden, Luke tells us, was so intense "his sweat was as ...great drops of blood falling...to the ground." (Luke 22:44.) He suffered an agony and a burden the like of which no human person would be able to bear. In that hour of anguish our Savior overcame all the power of Satan.

"During those days of unconsciousness I was given, by the gift and power of the Holy Ghost, a more perfect knowledge of His mission, I was also given a more complete understanding of what it means to exercise, in His name, the authority to unlock the mysteries of the kingdom of heaven for the salvation of all who are faithful. My soul was taught over and over again the events of the betrayal, the mock trial, the scouring of the flesh of even one of the Godhead. I witnessed His struggling up the hill in His weakened condition carrying the cross and His being stretched upon it as it lay on the ground, that the crude spikes could be driven with a mallet into His hands and wrists and feet to secure His body as it hung on the cross for public display.

"Crucifixion – the horrible and painful death which He suffered – was chosen from the beginning. By that excruciating death, He descended below all things, as is recorded, that through His resurrection He would ascend above all things. (See D&C 88:6)

"Jesus Christ died in the literal sense in which we will all die. His body lay in the tomb. The immortal spirit of Jesus, chosen as the Savior of mankind, went to those myriads of spirits who had departed mortal life with varying degrees of righteousness to God's laws."

In closing Elder David B. Haight said, "I cannot begin to convey to you the deep impact that these scenes have confirmed upon my soul . . . that most transcended of all events, the atoning sacrifice of our Lord."[3]

Later in my life I remember Elder Haight making a comment, "The pictures of Christ hanging upon the wall of our home and in church buildings are just pictures. He does not look like any of these pictures." This makes

---

[3] "The Sacrament – and the Sacrifice" by Elder David B. Haight, 1989 General Conference address.

perfect sense to me, after all he had a 'one-on-one' with the Savior for three days in the heavens above.

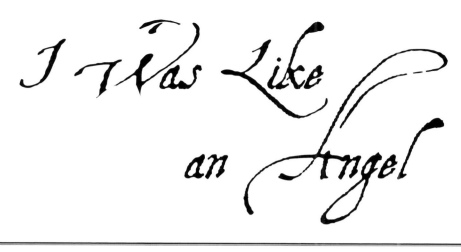

I Was Like an Angel

CHAPTER 8

Time marched on and on until my dad nearing the age of 90 years quietly crossed over into the world of spirits. He returned to his family farm.

Six months after dad passed, I experienced an out of body event. My spirit left my bedroom quickly into a very different realm or outer earth. There was no travel time, I was suddenly there. It was a beautiful place, something to behold.

As an angel, I found myself standing next to a very large tree along a spacious sidewalk with many trees and a variety of flowering tall bushes. The trees towered a hundred feet or more into the cloudless sky. The sun was very bright with an atmosphere above very pleasant which seemed to flower all about me. I thought why am I here? This is not my world. The sidewalk opened into a setting like a country park and my view expanded beyond.

On my left was a large three story house. It was towering very high with many windows. There was no one around. As I looked at the house it made me think of an old house in England. A house built for a very large family. The sidewalk was bordered with many flowering plants. There were blue skies, no clouds, and it was very peaceful. I felt very much at ease. At the back of the yard was a man dressed in farm coveralls with his back toward me. He was not aware of my presence. He was very busy sharpening a tool on an open work bench. To his right stood a tool shed and a well house with cool water flowing into a small reservoir with metal cans, similar to old milk cans, in the water.

The man at the work bench sensed my presence and turned toward me. It was my dad, Kenneth, dressed in his stripped coveralls with shoulder straps and a long sleeve farm shirt. He was surprised to see me. I was equally shocked to see him. No words were exchanged, just a short embrace and my visit was over. Dad looked content and happy. He had a full head of brown hair, his body appeared to be about thirty years of age and he had a broad smile from cheek to cheek. My dad was young and my appearance was older with my thinning hair which is gray-white. It was a different sort of visit. I was the visiting angel. And so ended my visit.

I Love You Mom

CHAPTER 9

In our day angelic activities are all around us. Yet many are unaware because their eyes are cloudy and their spirit lacks. Angels are co-workers with us; they communicate with us through a visitation, a voice, by thoughts, by feelings or many other ways.

Shortly after the passing of my mother Verla I received a call from heaven. I was down in spirit and my thoughts were upon her. At the time I was busy on a project in our home. The call came suddenly and quite unexpected.

I am almost totally deaf in my left ear. For years I wore a hearing aid then got tired of the whistling sounds, the battery replacements and the feeling of having a plug in my ear so I threw it away. The call came into my left ear, "Hi Howard, this is mom. I wanted to call. I'm so excited. Guess what? Shortly we are going to the county fair and it is something to behold. I'm so excited." Without notice the phone call was interrupted and sharply ended. Perhaps mom was breaking one of the heavenly rules.

Her voice sounded heavenly. I dropped to my knees, it was unbelievable and I pondered it for many days thereafter.

Angels may administer comfort, love or peace to us. Angels work with us in missionary service and provide protection. They assist us as we conduct work for the dead in our temples. In the words of Jeffery R. Holland, "One of the things that will become more important in our lives the longer we live is the reality of angels, their work and their ministry. I refer here not alone to the angel Moroni but also to those more personal ministering angels who are with us and around us, empowered to help us and who do exactly that."[1]

Just as my mother, angels are messengers and each who minister on this earth have belonged to it or may yet belong to it. Angels may be male or female. All angels are the offspring of God. Angels operate among children, women and men and are not a respecter of age, race or faith.

Joseph F. Smith shared, "When messengers are sent to minister to the inhabitants of this earth, they are not strangers, but from the ranks of our kindred, friends, and fellow beings and fellow servants."[2]

An LDS scholar, Robert L. Millet said, "An angel may be a resurrected being (D&C 129:1); a translated being; an unembodied spirit, one who has not yet taken a physical body; disembodied spirit, one who has lived, died and now awaits the resurrection; a mortal who is attentive to

---

[1] "For a Wise Purpose", Ensign, Jan. 1996, pp. 16-17
[2] Gospel Doctrine, 435.

the Spirit of God and follows divine direction to assist or bless another, or the Lord Himself."[3]

---

[3] "Angels in LDS Beliefs", p. 36; also see McConkie, Angels, pp. 11-23

A Suitcase of Good Deeds

CHAPTER 10

Our Eternal Father was not experimenting when this world came into existence. It did not come by chance. It is not the first of His creations. Millions upon millions of worlds such as this have rolled into existence before our earth was born.[1]

Why are we drawn towards certain persons, and they to us, as if we had always known each other? We believe that ties formed in this life will continue in the life to come; then why not believe that we had similar ties before we came into the world and that at least some of them have been resumed in this state of existence?

After meeting someone whom I had never met before in earth, I have wondered why that person's face seemed so familiar. The same is true of some strains of music, they are like echoes of eternity. When it comes to the gospel I feel more positive. Why did the Savior say: "My sheep know my voice?" Did a sheep ever know the voice of its shepherd if it had never heard that voice before? I believe

---

[1] Moses 1:33, 37-38

we knew the gospel before we came here, and that is what gives it a familiar sound.[2]

If Christ knew before hand so did we. But in coming here we forgot all, that our agency might be free indeed, to choose good or evil, that we might merit the reward of our own choice and conduct.[3]

Earth life is a short period of duration allotted to each of us called time. Sooner then we think life will be taken away; the lungs will cease to heave and the body will become lifeless. Is that the end of it or do we continue on? The spirit has only left the body.

Brigham Young said, "When the spirits of mankind leave their bodies, no matter whether the individual was a prophet or the meanest person that you could find, where do they go? To the spirit world."[4]

When we depart we carry a suitcase containing deeds recorded by our spirits whether good or bad during our housing an earthly body. Prepare your suitcase before death with good deeds and you'll have nothing to fear.

---

[2] 'The Way to Perfection' by Joseph Fielding Smith, 6th Edition, 1946, p. 45
[3] ERA magazine 23:101; Gospel Doctrine 15-16
[4] 'Temple of the Most High', p. 339; 'Place of Wicked Spirits and of the Spirit World', by Brigham Young, 'Excerpts of Discourse in the Bowery', SLC, Utah, June 22, 1856.

Strangers among Us

CHAPTER 11

Brigham Young, "Pretty soon you will see temples reared up, and the sons of Jacob will enter into the temple of the Lord. When you see Zion redeemed and built up – when you see the people performing the ordinances of salvation for themselves and for others . . . There will be strangers in your midst walking with you, talking with you.

"They will enter your houses, eat and drink with you as the Savior did with the two disciples who walked in the country in the days of old. They will expound the scriptures to you, and teach you of the resurrection of the just and the unjust, or the doctrine of salvation; and they will use the keys of the Holy Priesthood and unlock the doors of knowledge to let you look into the palace of truth. You will exclaim all is plain; why did I not understand it before? And you feel your heart burn within you as they walk and talk with you."[1]

---

[1] 'The Last Days', 6th Edition, by Robert W. Smith, July 1943, p. 45. 'Strangers to appear'. Also, 'Discourses of Brigham Young', Vol. VI, pp. 194-5 by Brigham Young.

Robert W. Smith in his writings share where men have come, spoken and vanished: A party on the way to Cedar City, Utah, by auto, recently picked up an aged man, and was deeply interested by his remarks. A puncture caused a delay. The men got out of the car and after the tire was changed, the driver looked for his passenger, but although there was an open stretch for miles in every direction, the old gentleman was not to be seen.[2]

A lady living on a lonely ranch was temporarily alone while her husband was on a trip to the city. She was taken ill and prayed for help. Shortly after a knock was heard, a kindly gentleman entered at her request. He stated that he had come to administer to her. He did so and she was immediately healed. After a short conversation, he stated that he would have to be on his way, stepped outside and closed the door. Feeling that she wished to again thank him the lady opened the door, but although she looked in every direction no one was to be seen.[3]

"A rumor is about that a gentleman arose and spoke in a Salt Lake meeting, with such a wealth of information that afterwards people stopped to talk with him, but he said he would have to leave, as he had a meeting to address in Pocatello, Idaho within an hour. He then left the building and his listeners marveled at this statement as Pocatello is many hours' drive away. Out of curiosity, one of the men present who was acquainted in the Pocatello Ward referred to, wrote and found that a man answering the

---

[2] 'The Last Days', 6th Edition, by Robert W. Smith, July 1943, p. 45.
[3] Ibid.

description of the stranger had spoken at the time set in that particular ward."[4]

A genealogical meeting was held on March 23, 1934 at the Eighth Ward, Liberty Stake (Utah). Melvin J. Ballard related the following experience and it is recorded in the minutes of that meeting. The Logan Temple was dedicated on 17 May, 1884; Melvin's father was one of those helping with its building and dedication. He being anxious to take names of his ancestors on opening day entered into correspondence with English relatives but without obtaining any names.

On the next day Melvin, then about ten years of age, was attending to his chores, when two gentlemen approached the house and spoke to two young girls, sisters to Melvin. One of the men handed the older of the two sisters a newspaper and told her to take it immediately to her father and to give it to none else.

The sisters came into the house about ready to enter the room where their father was holding a meeting with other brethren regarding the temple. Their mother forbade them saying father was not to be interrupted. However, when the girl stated that two gentlemen had given her a newspaper with explicit instructions that it was to be given immediately to her father, she was permitted to enter the room. Her father asked her what the men had said and where they were. The girls replied they were by the gate. He hastened to the window; although at the time Logan was sparsely settled with nothing to obscure their view for a block in either direction, yet the strangers were nowhere in sight.

---

[4] Statement of Brigham Young, 'Journal of Discourses', Vol. VI, pp. 194-195

Those assembled turned to the paper, to their surprise they found the date of the English paper was May 14, 1884, while the date received was May 18, 1884, making it but four days from England to Logan, Utah. It truly would have been impossible by any means of transportation known in those days.

Father Ballard turning the pages was surprised to find that an English reporter had been interested in particularly worded epitaphs on some old tombstones in a cemetery and had copied many of the names and dates, all of which proved to be relatives of the Ballard's; thus miraculously the names came in time for the work to be started on the opening day of the Logan Temple.

Melvin Ballard stated that this old newspaper is still preserved in the archives of the church.[5]

[5] "Genealogical Miracle", The Last Days, 6th Edition, by Robert W. Smith and Elizabeth A. Smith, July, 1943, pp. 46-47

A Stranger – One to Lean on

CHAPTER 12

In his personal history Joseph Smith tells us that Martin Harris began writing for him about April 12, 1828, and continued until June 14, 1828. Shortly thereafter 116 pages of the Book of Lehi had been translated. Martin Harris persisted that Joseph allow him to share this transcript of the Book of Mormon with his wife.

Joseph inquired of the Lord, received a first refusal and then a second refusal and finally an answer not like the two former ones. Martin Harris was permitted to take the manuscript home with him under certain conditions.

After three weeks and no report from Martin Harris, Joseph became very upset with himself yet kept his feelings from his wife. Finally he shared them with Emma and with her blessing he set out to find the missing Martin Harris and transcript. To make matters worse Joseph and Emma had just buried an infant son a few days earlier. This child, the eldest of Joseph and Emma, was born on June 15, 1828 and died on the same day.

Joseph set out on the first stage that passed for Palmyra and in the words of his mother, "And, although he was now nearly worn out, sleep fled from his eyes, neither had he any desire for food, for he felt that he had done wrong, and how great his condemnation was he did not know.[1]

"Only one passenger, a stranger, was in the stage with the prophet. He observed Joseph's gloomy appearance, inquired the cause of his affliction, and offered to assist him. Joseph mentioned his sick wife and child, that his son had died and his wife was still low; but refrained from giving any further explanation.

"Soon Joseph was about to leave the stage, at which time he remarked, 'That he still had twenty miles further to travel on foot by night, it being about ten o'clock.' The stranger said, 'I have watched you, I know that you have neither slept nor eaten since you entered the stage, and you shall not go on foot twenty miles alone this night; for, if you must go, I will be your company.'[2] Joseph thanked the stranger for his kindness and leaving the stage the two proceeded together and reached the house of Lucy Mack Smith at nearly daybreak. The stranger mentioned to Mother Smith that he was under the necessity of leading Joseph the last four miles by the arm. Joseph was too much exhausted to support himself any longer, and he would fall asleep as he was walking arm in arm along the way, toward the last of the distance.

"On entering our house, the stranger remarked that he had brought our son through the forest, because he had insisted on coming, that he was sick, and needed rest, as

---

[1] 'History of Joseph Smith' by His Mother Lucy Mack Smith, SLC, UT, 1945, p. 126
[2] Ibid., p. 127

well as refreshment, and that he ought to have some pepper tea to warm his stomach. After thus directing us, relative to our son, he said, 'that when we had attended to Joseph he would thank us for a little breakfast for himself, as he was in a haste to be on his journey again'.

"When Joseph had taken a little nourishment, according to the directions of the stranger, he requested us to send immediately for Mr. Harris. This we did without delay."[3]

Who was this stranger? Did he just happen by chance to be on the stage? The prophet Joseph was down in spirit, he had a sick wife, they had just buried a son, and had received no news from Martin Harris. Perhaps one of the Three Nephites was there to assist.

Moroni the son of Mormon wrote these words, "But behold, my father and I have seen them, and they have ministered unto us."[4] "And they are as the angels of God, and if they shall pray unto the Father in the name of Jesus they can show themselves unto whatsoever man it seemeth them good, therefore great and marvelous works shall be wrought by them, before the great and coming day when all the people must surely stand before the judgment seat of God; yea even among the Gentiles shall there be a great and marvelous work wrought by them before the judgment day."[5]

[3] Ibid., p. 127
[4] Mormon 8:10-11, 3 Nephi 25:26.
[5] 3 Nephi 28: 31-32

An Old Man Instantly Disappeared

CHAPTER 13

A man in his 30's, 40's, 50,'s or 60's is considered an old man to someone in his 20's. A man in his 80's or 90's is considered an old man to one in his 50's. A man with white hair and beard is considered old to a man in his 20's.

In September 1878 Joseph F. Smith and Orson Pratt paid a visit to David Whitmer at his home in Richmond, Missouri. He shared a testimony regarding the hill Cumorah and a stranger.

"When I was returning to Fayette, Joseph and Oliver attended with me all of us riding in a wagon. Oliver and I sat on an old-fashioned wooden spring seat and the Prophet Joseph sat behind us. While traveling across a clear open space, a very pleasant, nice-looking old man suddenly appeared by the side of our wagon and saluted us with, 'good morning, it is very warm', at the same time wiping his face and forehead with his hand. We returned the salutation . . . by a sign from Joseph, I invited him to ride if he was going our way; but he said very pleasantly, 'No, I am going to Cumorah'. This name was something new to me; I did not know what Cumorah meant. We all gazed at him and at each other, and as I looked around inquiringly of Joseph, the old man instantly disappeared, so that I did not see him again."

Joseph F. Smith then asked: "Did you notice his appearance?"

David Whitmer said: "I should think I did. He was, I should think, about five feet eight or nine inches tall and heavy set . . . His hair and beard were white, like brother Pratt's, but his beard was not so heavy. I also remember that he had on his back a sort of knapsack with something in it, shaped like a book."[1]

Wayne May, a noted archaeologist, has more knowledge in one finger than most men retain in ten fingers regarding the ancients of America. Wayne has walked, studied, climbed and visited hundreds of Indian mounds, many times with other experts in this field of work. He has addressed thousands of people spanning a period of over thirty years across this great country of America. Recently he visited the land of the dinosaur in Vernal, Utah.

Wayne spoke at a Book of Mormon Evidence Conference and centered his talk on the hill Cumorah. Giving credit to Apostle Orson Pratt he said, "The hill Cumorah with the surrounding vicinity, is distinguished as the great battle field on which two powerful nations were concentrated with all their forces. Men, women and children all fought until hundreds of thousands on both

---

[1] 'Doctrine of Salvation', p. 237. Also, 'Ancient America, Archaeology of the America's Before Columbus', by Wayne N. May, LDS Special Edition VI, Fall 2013.

sides were hewn down and left to molder upon the ground. Both armies were Israelites; both had become awfully corrupt, having apostatized from God. The Nephites, as a nation, became extinct; the Lamanites alone were left. This happened, according to their faithful records, near the close of the fourth century of the Christian era. The American Indians are remnants of the once powerful nation of Lamanites.

"The hill Cumorah is remarkable also as being the hill on which and around which a still more ancient nation perished, called the Jaredites. This unparalleled destruction is recorded in the Book of Ether, and happened about six centuries before Christ. The Jaredites colonized America from the tower of Babel. After about sixteen centuries, during which they became exceedingly numerous, through their terrible wars they destroyed themselves. The hill Cumorah, by them, was called Ramah. Millions fought against millions, until the hill Ramah and the land around was soaked with blood, and their carcasses were left in countless numbers to molder back to mother earth. (Orson Pratt, *Millennial Star*, Vol. 28, 417-419)"[2]

Remember . . . the old man with a knapsack and something in it shaped like a book instantly disappearing.

---

[2] 'Ancient America, Archaeology of the America's Before Columbus', by Wayne N. May, LDS Special Edition VI, Fall 2013.

The Ice Closed Behind 'Us'

CHAPTER 14

Shortly after the organization of the Church Joseph Smith received a revelation from the Lord on January 2, 1831, commanding him to move members of the church to Kirtland, Ohio.[1] Some left by way of land. Joseph and Emma Smith, Sidney Rigdon and Edward Partridge traveled in a sleigh provided by Joseph Knight. This group arrived on a snowy and cold February 2, 1831 gathering at the Gilbert-Whitney store in Kirtland.[2]

Members of the Colesville branch and others traveled by way of water. Lucy Mack Smith, a lady of beauty and intelligence, organized a party of twenty adults and thirty children to travel by barge on the Cayuga and Seneca Canal to Buffalo, New York. Then by steam boat on Lake Erie to Fairport, Ohio. It was late February and it was not an easy task. The lake was frozen over and impassable. Fairport is twelve miles northeast of Kirtland.

---

[1] D & C 38:32
[2] History of the Church 1:146-146; also see Elizabeth Ann Whitney's account in 'They Knew the Prophet' by Hyrum and Helen Mae Andus, Bookcraft 1974, p. 39

At Buffalo, under Lucy's direction, the luggage trunks are loaded onto the ship and stacked up high and all individuals board the ship. The ship appears to be overloaded, people on the shoreline are very concerned that it just might sink in the harbor. The lake was frozen – yet it was the only pathway.

Lake Erie is the shallowest of all the Great Lakes yet also the warmest by summer end. Late February usually is the time for the winter ice to break up however not this year. It is a dangerous lake, "the lightest breeze can kick up lively waves". Many ships over time have reached the bottom.[3]

At departure mother Smith stood holding onto the ship's deck rail bidding farewell to those gathered on the dock. Just then a stranger on the shoreline cried out, "Is the Book of Mormon true?" Mother Smith standing very erect with the light of Christ upon her delivered a very powerful testimony for all to hear. She spoke with authority as if called from God. In the voice of an angel the prophet's mother cried out, "That book, replied I, was brought forth by the power of God and translated by the gift of the Holy Ghost; and, if I could make my voice sound as loud as the trumpet of Michael, the Archangel, I would declare the truth from land to land, and from sea to sea, and the echo should reach to every isle, until every member of the family of Adam should be left without excuse."[4]

The crowd gathered along the shore are gravely concerned. How can this overloaded ship break through

[3] http://en.wikipedia.org/wiki/Lake_Erie/Ferryboats, see item #25.
[4] 'History of the Church 1': p. 204; also 'History of Joseph Smith' by His Mother Lucy Mack Smith; comments by Preston Nibley, SLC, 1945, p. 204

the ice? This ship is a replica of 'Walk in the Water' built in Buffalo, New York around 1816. It is a very sturdy ship, nevertheless, the captain is facing some very serious concerns. One, can this ship possibly break through the ice cap without serious damage; and two, will the passengers be safe? Yet the captain fires up the steam engine.

Oh! The faith of mother Smith standing on the deck, lifting her arms towards heaven and said, "Now brethren and sisters, if you will all raise your desires to heaven that the ice may be broken up, and we set at liberty, as sure as the Lord lives, it will be done." At that instant a noise was heard like bursting thunder. All along the shoreline felt the bursting thunder.[5] The captain yells out, 'Everyone to his post.' The ice parted, leaving a passage just wide enough for the ship.

Can anyone picture the chill in the air, noise of thunder and shaking of the ship as it left the dock?

Lucy Mack Smith, "We had barely passed through the avenue when the ice closed behind us and the saints from the Colesville branch were left in Buffalo, unable to follow us. As we were leaving the harbor, one by-stander exclaimed, 'There goes the Mormon company! That boat is sunk in the water nine inches deeper than ever it was before, and mark it, she will sink – there is nothing surer.' Little did this man know about the children of light, "In fact, they (those with him) were so sure of it that they went straight to the Buffalo News printing office and reported that we were sunk, so that when we arrived at Fairport we read in the paper news of our own death." For

---

[5] Ibid, p. 205

those days the news carried fast. Could it be possible Joseph, Hyrum and others also heard of this news and with action headed to Fairport with anticipation of just not knowing?

A Stranger in Wait

CHAPTER 15

After Buffalo, the ship captain made several stops along the way. The ship hung to the south side of Lake Erie making it much easier to plow through the ice. Lucy Mack Smith was unaware that a stranger was on the shoreline at Fairport in wait for three days. More than likely he was doing a little fishing.

Mother Smith shared her travel itinerary of this journey, "After our miraculous escape from the wharf at Buffalo, we called our company together and had a prayer meeting in which we offered up our thanks to God for his mercy, which he had manifested towards us in our deliverance . . . Soon after leaving Buffalo, some of our company begin to feel the effects of the motion of the boat, and were overcome with sea-sickness. I went to the cook, and, handing him twenty-five cents, asked him if he could let me have some hot water for the sick folks. He complied with my request and I was thus furnished with the means of making them comfortable."[1]

Speaking of the ship's captain Lucy said, "Upon further acquaintance with the captain, I made myself known to him as the sister of General Mack. Smiling he seemed highly pleased to find in me a relative of his old friend. I was treated with great respect, both by himself and crew, while I remained on the boat."[2]

Oh! The light of mother Smith. In the words of Craig C. Christensen, "As you let your light shine, others . . . will be inspired by you to seek greater light." He said, "Children of the light do not sit passively in darkness; they have the courage to stand up and stand out. When the adversary comes looming, children of the light know when to fight back, when to say no and when to simply walk away."[3]

Drawing near Fairport the captain prepared the ship to land. Fairport was a port of call for boats carrying immigrants from Europe, going to the upper lakes regions, and a haven of calm water for boats in a storm. An ideal spot for a stranger to wait.

Mother Smith said, "Nearing where we were to land, the captain, passengers, and crew bade me farewell in tears. After landing, our company were more disheartened than ever, and the brethren came round me and requested that I should set their wives to sewing blankets together,

---

[1] 'History of Joseph Smith by His Mother, Lucy Mack Smith', SLC, UT, 1945, p. 205.
[2] Ibid, p. 206
[3] Church News, Week of March 24, 2013, p.15, Elder Craig C. Christensen speaks on 'Becoming Children of Light' given at a Devotional at BYU-Idaho.

and making tents for them, that the men might camp by their goods and watch over them, for they had no hope of getting any further. I told them I should do nothing of the kind.

"As I passed among them, my attention was attracted by a stranger, who sat a short distance from us on the shore on the lake. I inquired of him the distance to Kirtland. He, standing up, exclaimed, 'Is it possible that this is Mother Smith? I have sat here looking for you these three days.'

"Replying to his question in the affirmative, I asked him if it would be possible to procure teams to take our goods to Kirtland. He told me to give myself no uneasiness about the matter. That Joseph was expected in the hour, and in less than twenty four hours there would be teams sufficient to take all our company to houses that were waiting to receive them.

"When he mentioned Joseph's name, I startled, for I just began to realize that I was so soon to see both my husband and my sons. I turned away from the stranger and Samuel was coming toward me, closely followed by Joseph. I extended my right hand to Samuel and my left to Joseph. They wept for joy upon seeing me.

"Samuel wept, because he had been warned of God in a dream to meet the company from Waterloo, and feared some disaster had befallen me; and Joseph because of the information which he had received that he apprehended, from the fatigue I was undergoing, my life was in danger.[4]"

---

[4] 'History of Joseph Smith by His Mother Lucy Mack Smith', SLC, UT, 1945, pp. 206-207

The stranger was no longer. Powers and abilities of the Three Nephites are sometimes unbelievable to mortals for we see out of clay eyes. "They can show themselves unto whatsoever man it seemeth them good."[5] Lucy Mack Smith saw the stranger on the shoreline while others did not.

Melvin J. Ballard commented, "Although they have the ability to live in the earth among men, they have power over the elements of earth, power over the law of gravitation, by which they could move over the face of the earth with the speed of their own thoughts, power to reveal themselves to men and yet power to mingle and move among men unobserved and hidden."[6]

---

[5] 3 Nephi 28:30
[6] Address by Elder Melvin J. Ballard, The Path to Celestial Happiness, spoken on October 25, 1925, as printed in the Deseret News, Oct. 31, 1925.

Three Nephites Armed for Battle

CHAPTER 16

The City of Enoch, the Lost Ten Tribes, the Three Nephites, John the Revelator, and others over time have been given power to overcome the elements.[1]

One of their powers is the ability to be transported from place to place instantaneously. We are now entering a day of understanding. Some have the eyes to meet them, shake hands and know of their presence and feel of their spirit.

While making his way to the church office building with President Joseph Fielding Smith, Harold B. Lee expressed: "I believe there has never been a moment of time since the creation but what there has been someone holding the priesthood on the earth to hold Satan in check. And then I thought of Enoch's city with perhaps thousands who were taken into heaven and were translated. They have been translated for a purpose and

---

[1] John 21: 22-23; Book of Mormon 3 Nephi 28:5-7

may have sojourned with those living on the earth since that time."[2]

Jesus speaking of John the Divine said, "If I will that he tarry till I come, what is that to thee?"[3] Clarification comes on to the position of John, "Thou shalt tarry until I come in my glory, and shall prophesy before nations, kindreds, tongues, and people."[4]

The Lord speaking to the Three Nephites said, "Behold I know your thoughts, and ye have desired the thing which John, my beloved, who was with me in my ministry, before that I was lifted up by the Jews, desired of me." Speaking to the twelve, nine of them replied, "We desire that after we have lived unto the age of man, that our ministry wherein thou has called us, may have an end that we may speedily come unto thee in thy kingdom."[5]

Yet the Three Nephite disciples desiring the greater to remain, to spend their days working among the people and at times go unnoticed by others. Because of their desire the Lord had in store for them such blessings to which we have no way of comprehending.

In Missouri during 1835 new problems erupted between the Mormons and their neighbors when the saints began to settle in the counties surrounding Caldwell, including DeWitt in Carroll County and Adam-ondi-Ahman or Spring Hill in Daviess County. A series of escalating conflicts followed the Governor of Missouri, he eventually

---

[2] Address given July 8, 1964, 'Stand Ye in Holy Places', 'Selected Sermons and Writing of President Harold B. Lee', Deseret Book, 1974, p. 161
[3] John 21:22
[4] D&C 7:3
[5] Book of Mormon, 3 Nephi 28:1-8

called out twenty five hundred state militia men "to put down the Mormon rebellion". The Latter-day Saints poured into Far West for protection and found themselves under siege. It is known as the Mormon War.[6]

From the journal of Oliver B. Huntington, "On the 30th of October 1838 a large company of armed soldiers, were seen approaching Far West . . . October 31 Mormon militia guarded the city the past night . . . with fortifications of wagons, timber, on the south . . . the enemy was five to one against us. The army came on, near the spot designated and on a sudden they all turned and ran pel mell (sic) back to their camp, in great fright, declaring they saw too many thousands of soldiers to think of attacking the city."

Joseph Smith said, "That he saw between them and the mob one of the Three Nephites, with a drawn sword just before he made the remark about opening fire upon them, and when the mob had returned he saw the Three Nephites near the same place armed for battle.

"The host that the Three Nephites had with them, were undoubtedly exposed by the power of God, to the view of the mob, being hosts of soldiers they saw and fled from."[7]

And in our day, 'Wo unto him that spurneth at the doings of the Lord, wo unto him that shall deny the Christ and his works! Yea, wo unto him that shall deny the revelations of the Lord and that shall say the Lord no longer worketh by revelation, or by prophecy, or by gifts,

[6] http://en.m.wikipedia.org/wiki/Far_West_Missouri
[7] 'Oliver B. Huntington, His Personal History', pp. 5-6, which is housed at B.Y.U. Collection Library

or by tongues, or by healings, or by the power of the Holy Ghost.'[8]

Yes! Translated beings are among us in our day mightily at work; occasionally one may just go fishing sitting on the shoreline of Lake Erie waiting and waiting for Mother Smith.

---

[8] Book of Mormon, 3 Nephi 29:5-6

An Open Vision

CHAPTER 17

Beginning at Richmond, then Liberty Jail, Joseph and Hyrum's internment seemed to drag on and on – never ending – from November 1, 1838 to April 15, 1839. Then finally the escape.

At Liberty Jail, the two sons of Lucy Mack Smith were kept under heavy guard living in a filthy, damp, cold, thick walled small enclosure of a one room building of no size. A room not fit for chickens to lay eggs or for any other animal. A bucket with a rope was used to lower the food, mostly unfit for human consumption, and a bucket as a toilet to serve the needs of several men. Wintertime in Missouri was extremely cold, no heat, and just a small opening for light.

In early April news of a new trial and a meeting with Judge Austin A. King was to be held in Daviess County, Missouri. Under guard the prisoners arrived on April 9th wherein Joseph and Hyrum are now indicted for "murder, treason, burglary, arson, larceny, theft and stealing", all drummed up charges worthy of death.[1] Of course all these charges are false and none of these men had performed such acts. On the 16th of April the prisoners start for Boone County. During the move Joseph, Hyrum and others make their escape.[2]

The night before the escape, Lucy Mack Smith has an open vision or dream regarding her sons. She is staying at the Cleveland farmhouse along with Emma Smith and her family hoping someday for the return of Joseph and Hyrum.

In her vision, Lucy saw her two sons Joseph and Hyrum in travel. They were ragged, very tired, hungry and with but one horse. Lucy said, "I saw them stop, tie their horse to a stump of a burnt sapling, then lie down on the ground to rest themselves, and they looked so pale and faint that it distressed me. I sprang up and said to my husband, 'Oh, Mr. Smith, I can see Joseph and Hyrum and they are so weak they can hardly stand. Now they are lying on the cold ground asleep! Oh how I wish that I could give them something to eat!'"[3] Hyrum and Joseph reached Quincy, Illinois, April 23, 1839.[4] Lucy continues, "The next day I made preparation to receive my sons, confident that the poor, afflicted wanderers would arrive at home before noon."[5] To which they did.

The Cleveland farm (authors' family tree) is located four miles out of Quincy, Illinois. Emma, her children, and some or all of the Rigdon family, made up a portion of the

---

[1] History of the Church 3:315
[2] History of the Church 3:321 – In an affidavit by Hyrum Smith, the 'escape' is fully described.
[3] Lucy Mack Smith, op. cit., pp 301-302.
[4] The Relief Society Magazine, Vol. III. No. 3.
[5] Lucy Mack Smith, op. cit., pp 301-302

household. . . A ragged, dirty, emaciated Joseph Smith approached the yard gate of the Cleveland house. It is early morning on April 24; a family member saw Emma look out the door, and rushed outdoors into Joseph's arms. The prophet barely made it halfway up the path to the house."[6]

---

[6] 'A Mighty Welcome by All'. Dimick B. Huntington statement, LDS Archives. As quoted in David E. Miller and Della S. Miller, 'Nauvoo: The City of Joseph', p. 26.

Kinnikinick

CHAPTER 18

"My nickname is Kinnikinick. And in my youth almost all my friends went barefooted, not because it was a way of life, our feet got very tough. I knew all the trails and shortcuts between Centerville and Farmington Utah. I can't remember cutting my feet.

"By late summer I was tan like an Indian, barefooted and working my dad's farm. In 1915 our town was around 400 people most were produce farmers. Sagebrush separated the landscape of the farms with pathways between them. From our place I could view the water of the Great Salt Lake just a short distance to the west.

"Along the lake's edge the cattails grew tall towering over my head and it is a favorite spot for duck and geese. I shot many a duck and goose. Huge carp made their way along the edges and with my bow and arrow with string I was ready for a tug-of-war.

"Kinnikinick is the name of the sumac willow. The leaves of this willow was smoked by American Indians. I imagined myself a great hunter. At the base of the Rocky

77

Mountains from our farm I walked up to the mouth of Centerville Canyon and Duel Creek and cut Kinnikinick for bows and flipper sticks. I would go west toward the lake and cut cattails for arrows. I would balance the arrows by pushing a shingle nail into the heavy end. These arrows would carry out for a full distance."

Around 1950, my dad taught me the trade of cutting sumac willow, cattails, and making bow and arrows. I was fitted up ready for a hunt. He also taught me how to make flippers and slingshots. He explained, "Son, you take two long cow hide strips and tie them to a leather pouch the size of your small hand." He then selected a rock that was very smooth and oval shape. "The accuracy of the slingshot is in the selection of the rock. A rock with rough edges, somewhat out of shape, will go nowhere and will miss the target."

Kenneth Carlos Smith an avid fisherman made many pathways along Farmington Creek, Duel Creek, and the Weber River. The Weber River was noted for large native cutthroats, red throat suckers, and large whitefish. Farmington Creek was loaded with small rainbow and cutthroats. My mother would dust the smaller trout with flour, season with salt and pepper then fried quickly in butter making quite a treat. The skin is a tasty part of the fish. She would top it off with homemade bread and a glass of whole milk.

From dad's journal, "Anyone acquainted with me knows I have always enjoyed hunting ducks, geese, deer, pheasants and other game birds until I became 65 years of age. I always liked to fish and I'm still an active fisherman at 71 years soon 72. I especially like stream fishing. Most men my age won't fish the streams, they fish the lakes which is not as strenuous. I hope I can stumble around for a few more years and fish the streams."

Dad had a love for the gospel with a personal testimony of Jesus Christ. He was baptized December 1913 in a wooden horse trough in Centerville, Utah. Snow was on the ground and the water was ice cold. He was ordained a Seventy by J. Golden Kimball and a High Priest July 1974 in Layton, Utah.

Stumbling along nearing age 90, dad was like a large rock in a river that didn't wash away; with time its rough edges were worn smooth and polished. Before crossing over, he left a blessing upon the family.

Footprints in the Snow

CHAPTER 19

In my father's journal he states, "In my days as a lad, Farmington Creek was loaded from the tops of the mountains on down several thousand feet to the bottom lands with many catchable rainbow and native cutthroat fish. A limit was a krill full, the stream water was ice cold and fish just didn't grow large. Fish average 7 to 12 inches. One could point your head anywhere into the creek and drink refreshing ice cold mineral like water. It was my favorite creek for wet fly fishing."

On an early March day (1930's), dad made his way up the snow covered dirt road to the flatland of Farmington Creek. A fresh white snow had blanketed the area, the scrub oak trees were decorated in snow. The only tracks were from the car tires and dad's boot prints. It was a wonderland, a blue day, bright sun, just the kind of day to get away and be by yourself.

Dad was sporting his hip boots, fly rod, krill basket, a light jacket and a brim hat to do a little fly fishing. No one was around. At the age of 26 he was a young man enjoying the outdoors.

From his stance the tall majestic Rocky Mountains stood above him. Just below dad could view many miles of flat land lying between the small town of Farmington, Centerville and the Great Salt Lake. To the southwest his view extended to West Bountiful. Unbeknownst to him the Legion sword of the prophet Joseph Smith was hidden away.

Quoting my dad, "The fish just weren't biting. Deep in thought, I was suddenly shaken when a voice out of nowhere said, 'Good morning sir, how is the fishing?' The stranger was dressed like it was a summer day, his shorts revealed his lower legs, he was wearing boots, a long sleeve shirt and a large brim hat."

"He said, 'This is one of my favorite fishing spots. Do you mind if I fish for a little bit downstream?' 'No problem.' I extended my hand in friendship.

"A few yards downstream the man with almost every cast pulled in a fish. Within a short time a stringer of trout was on a forked willow stick. He was soon walking up stream with a friendly smile and approached me. He said, "I must be on my way. Would you like to have the stringer of trout?" 'Thank you. Are you sure?' He said "Yes". Again I said 'Thank you.' He then walked off through the snow. I look down at the catch. Looking up he was gone. I followed his footprints a short distance. Surprisingly his footprints vanished."

Dad shared this experience with me while fishing this same spot years later. This is highly unusual for dad as he hardly shared any stories with me regarding dreams or unexplainable occurrences. It was imprinted upon my mind – and now onto paper.

City of Enoch –
Zion is Fled

CHAPTER 20

What would it be like to visit the ancient city of Enoch? Was it a real place with real people? The Book of Enoch is among the lost books of the Holy Bible. Much of what we know about Enoch was restored by the Prophet Joseph Smith and is a part of the Pearl of Great Price.

Enoch built a city that was called the City of Holiness, even Zion. The Lord calls His people Zion a people with one mind, one heart, no poor among them and they dwelt in righteousness . . . And from thence went forth the saying, Zion is fled.[1]

Deliberate wickedness of the people in Enoch's time created a moral turbulence that was reflected in chaotic nature – earthquakes, tidal waves and cosmic cataclysms. Against this stormy background stands the commanding figure of Enoch. The prophet, who held the keys to a dispensation and probed the mysteries of God through his visions of the creation, the destiny of man, and the mission of the Savior. From the power of that faith and

---

[1] Moses 7:69

visions came the city of Enoch, a society that achieved the seemly impossible dream of being truly just, truly peaceful. In its achievement and its departure, it planted the seeds of hope for the righteous societies that followed it including that of our generation.[2]

Noah is the great grandson of Enoch. In Noah's time men had quickly reached the point of no return. The time line ran out and Noah pleaded for the lives to whom he had tried to reform; this included many of his extended family. The people became ripe like rotten fruit into iniquity.

The Lord spoke to Noah saying, "My spirit shall not always strive with man . . . and if men do not repent, I will send in the floods upon them."[3]

Picture in your mind cities buried under mountains of water with millions of dead bodies tossed about by the watery waves. This deluge of water upon the earth destroyed the wicked and also baptized mother earth from the sins placed upon it. It was a big event.

John the Baptist standing in the river Jordan baptizing scores of people declared, "I indeed baptize you with water, but one mightier than I cometh, the latchet of whose shoes I am not worthy to unloose; he shall baptize you with the Holy Ghost and with fire."[4] Mother earth was baptized in Noah's day just as John the Baptist was baptizing the saints of his day under water in the river Jordan.

---

[2] June 1977, 'A Strange Thing in the Land: The Return of the Book of Enoch. Part 12', by Hugh Nibley.
[3] Moses 8:17
[4] Luke 3:16

Enoch was ordained to the priesthood when he was twenty-five years of age.[5] When the Lord called him to be a prophet he hesitated to accept the call because he was "a lad" and hated because he was "slow of speech".[6] Nevertheless the Lord healed Enoch of his impediment and he became a mighty prophet, seer and revelator.

Enoch moved mountains from their place at his command; rivers actually turned from their course; the very earth trembled "so great was the power of the language which God had given him."[7]

Enoch built a great city of which he later defended as a valiant general.[8] Was Enoch scholarly in his ability to listen, take notes, and write? Yes . . . He was the clerk of the conference called by Adam and held at Adam-ondi-Ahman. Enoch wrote the official record of this conference and placed it into a book along with other information. This written compilation became known as the Book of Enoch.[9]

(Enoch) . . . But before that day he saw great tribulations among the wicked; and he also saw the sea, that it was troubled, and men's hearts failing them, looking forth with fear for the judgments of the Almighty God, which should come upon the wicked.[10]

---

[5] 'D & C 107:48
[6] Moses 6:31
[7] Moses 7:18
[8] Moses 7:13
[9] D & C 107:57
[10] Pearl of Great Price, Moses 7:66

And the Lord showed Enoch all things, even unto the end of the world; and he saw the day of the righteous, the hour of their redemption, and received a fullness of joy.[11]

And all the days of Zion, in the days of Enoch, were three hundred and sixty-five years.[12]

And Enoch and all his people walked with God, and he dwelt in the midst of Zion; and it came to pass that Zion was not, for God received it up into his own bosom; and from thence went forth the saying, 'Zion is fled'.[13]

Enoch was age 430 when he and all his city were translated; a large piece of land above and below the sea moved from mother earth through space to another sphere of motion.[14] Undisturbed these people, their homes, streets, churches, temples, families – young and old, along with their work places left this world.

Enoch and his people are looking forward to the Second Coming of Jesus Christ, anticipating the millennium. To them it is a big event, a return to this earth, a thousand years of peace.

Joseph Fielding Smith speaks of our day with this event not too far into the future and many things lie at our door steps. Soon all people will be tested and the earth cleansed just like the floods in Noah's time cleansed the earth. At this time or shortly after the burning and destruction of the wicked, Enoch and his translated city

---

[11] Pearl of Great Price, Moses 7:67
[12] Pearl of Great Price, Moses 7:68
[13] Pearl of Great Price, Moses 7:69
[14] Moses 7:21, 69

will return back to this planet in accordance with the promise of the Lord.[15]

---

[15] 'Teachings of the Prophet Joseph Smith, by Joseph Fielding Smith', 1938, Deseret News Press, pp. 170-172.

A Stranger by the Roadside

CHAPTER 21

Below is an interview with Homer M. Brown, Patriarch of the Granite Stake (Utah) and grandson of Mr. and Mrs. Benjamin Brown who gave refuge to the Prophet Joseph Smith several times.

"Brother Brown, Did the prophet ever tell your grandfather about the city of Enoch being taken from the earth? Yes, he did. He said that Enoch and his people kept so faithfully the law of the Lord, that they were translated. Not only Enoch and his people, but the great city wherein they dwelt. And Grandfather asked questions: Brother Joseph, where is the city of Enoch located? And the prophet answered, Where the Gulf of Mexico now exists. And he said the time will come when the mariner will say, there is not a bottom to the Gulf of Mexico, and he said when the great piece of land was taken from the earth, it created a vacuum, and to the extent that it started water coming in to fill up that great space that is now known as the Gulf Stream. The prophet added, In consequence of this great portion being taken it naturally threw the earth out of balance. Now, he said, when that comes back, that and the planet on which the lost tribes are, the earth will receive its equilibrium, and will revolve as it naturally was."[1]

The city of Enoch is somewhere in space, more than likely attached to another planet of considerable size. A terrestrial planet with translated beings. What part will Enoch's people and other translated beings play as we approach the Second Coming? Are they among us today? Just who are these strangers in our mist?

Brigham Young made a statement regarding the "Signs of the Millennium" and strangers among us in our day. "Pretty soon you will see temples reared up, and the sons of Jacob will enter into the Temples of the Lord. When you see Zion redeemed and built up – when you see the people performing the ordinances of salvation for themselves and for others . . . there will be strangers in your midst walking with you, talking with you; they will enter your houses and eat and drink with you, go to meetings with you, and begin to open your minds, as the Savior did the two disciples who walked out in the country in the days of old. About the time the temples are ready, the strangers will be along and will converse with you, and will inquire of you probably if you understand the resurrection of the dead. They will expound the scriptures to you, and open your minds, and teach you of the resurrection of the just and the unjust, or the doctrine of salvation; they will use the keys of the holy priesthood, and unlock the door of knowledge, to let you look into the palace of truth. You will exclaim, that it is all plain: why did I not understand it before? And you will

---

[1] 'The Last Days', by Robert W. Smith, 6th Edition, 1943, pp. 217-218

begin to feel your heart burn within you as they walk and talk with you.[2]"

Joseph Smith received several visits from translated beings; one happened on the journey with Zion's Camp. ". . . while 'the camp of Zion was on the way to Missouri in 1834, Joseph was ahead of the company one day, when there was seen talking with him by the roadside a man, a stranger. When the company came up there was no person with him. When at camp that night, Heber C. Kimball asked the prophet who that man was; Joseph replied it was the beloved Disciple, John, who was then on his way to the Ten Tribes in the north."[3]

Bruce R. McConkie comments: "Some mortals have been translated. In this state, they are not subject to sorrow or to disease or to death . . . procreation ceases. If they then had children, their offspring would be denied a mortal probation, which all worthy spirits must receive in due course. They have power to move and live in both a mortal and an unseen sphere. All translated beings undergo another change in their bodies when they gain full immortality. This change is the equivalent of a resurrection."[4]

[2] 'Signs of the Millennium', "Strangers To Appear", Statement of Brigham Young (Journal of Discourses., Vol. VI, pgs. 194-5)
[3] 'Personal History, Oliver B. Huntington', P.5., BYU Collection Library.
[4] 'The Millennial Messiah', Deseret Book, by Bruce R. McConkie, 1982, p. 644.

A Canoe at Massacre Point

CHAPTER 22

There is a revelation given by the Lord through His Prophet Joseph Smith on the bank of the Missouri River, McIlwaine's Bend, on August 12, 1831. On their return trip to Kirtland, Ohio the prophet and the elders had traveled down the Missouri River in canoes. On the third day of the journey, many dangers were experienced. William W. Phelps, in a daylight vision, saw the destroyer riding in power upon the face of the waters.[1]

In this revelation the Lord said, "But verily I say unto you, that it is not needful for this whole company of mine elders to be moving swiftly upon the waters, whilst the inhabitants on either side are perishing in unbelief. . . . Nevertheless, I suffered it that ye might bear record; behold, there are many dangers upon the waters, and more especially hereafter. . . . For I the Lord, have

---

[1] D & C Section 61, 'dangers upon the waters'

decreed in mine anger many destructions upon the waters; yea, and especially upon these waters.[2]

My thoughts are that spirit beings can skim across a river similar to when you have a fly pole in hand and with a back loop effect cast a light line with an attached dry fly out across the surface allowing the fly to hop and skip attracting a large fish. A spirit can go across any river with speed, without any effort or fear of drowning. Similar to a dry fly the spirit being does not get wet.

As mortals we are like a threaded worm on a hook and a sinker attached to the line all these hit the surface and without any effort sink to the bottom. With no effort to resurface, our spirit will soon separate from our mortal body then we too are spirit angels. The spirit being will resurface then skip across the river. Hopefully a friend or relative will be there to greet and welcome you home.

On a warm sunny day at Massacre Point, in late September around noon I was casting a bright silver spoon out into the river. From my vantage point I spot what appears to be a canoe making its way upstream with ease, it seems to be flowing across the river. My binoculars are with me so with a slight adjustment I'm able to look upon the canoe.

This person appears to be a very large Native American with paddle in hand gracefully making his way up the river on the opposite side. The current is strong yet there was no struggle on the part of the individual in the canoe. This man is large, over seven feet tall, his head is twice as large as mine and he has thick black hair hanging well over his shoulders. He is solidly built yet paddling in a

---

[2] Ibid, verses 3-5

small canoe with ease. The Indian has very dark skin. He circles the canoe toward the rivers center then toward me. The current did not pull it down stream.

Standing tall on the fishing dock I yelled out "Hi." Still a distance off the Indian hollered out "Hi, how's the fishing?" I almost fell off the fishing ramp, it was the voice of a lady in a giant body. She spoke with a heavenly voice. She was turning the canoe to head back down stream. I offered her water and a sandwich. She said, "Thank you, but I have a lunch and water with me."

She was very friendly. I asked her where she was from. She said, "I'm from western New York, I'm out here to visit a friend in Idaho. "I've always wanted to canoe the Snake River. Wow, what a river! Back home I canoe all the time along the Atlantic sea. It's a hobby. The sea is my favorite spot." I watched as she circled across the river again to the west side paddling gracefully downstream very quickly. Soon the canoe disappeared from my sight.

Who was this woman? She appeared to be of Native American descent, in a small canoe which seemed considerably old for our day. Why did she circle the canoe toward me yet hold her position in the center of the river while we talked? To this day I'm still trying to understand and reason it out. Could she possibly be an angel?

America is The Land

CHAPTER 23

A friend, Rod Meldrum said, "The Book of Mormon is a record of the forefathers of our western tribes of Indians . . . by it we learn our western tribes are descendants from that Joseph that was sold into Egypt, and the land of America is a promised land unto them.

"Few realize that some of the oldest, largest and most complex structures of ancient archaeology were built of earth, clay, and stone right here in America, in the Ohio and Mississippi valleys."[1]

Brigham Young states, "This is the land of Zion. West of us is a body of water that we call the Pacific, and to the east there is another large body of water which we call the Atlantic, and to the north is where they have tried to discover a Northway passage; these waters surround the land of Zion."[2]

---

[1] 'The Book of Mormon in America's Heartland' by Rod L. Meldrum, June 2011, p. 9 and p. 26. www.BookofMormonEvidence.org
[2] 'Discourses of Brigham Young', by John A Widsow Deseret Book Company, Salt Lake City Utah, 1966 p. 119

"There is a curse on the aborigines of our country who roamed the plains, and are so wild that you cannot tame them. They are of the house of Israel; they once had the gospel delivered to them, they had the oracles of truth; Jesus came to them and administered to them after his resurrection, and they received and delighted in the gospel until the fourth generation when they turned away and became so wicked that God cursed them with a dark and benighted and loathsome condition."[3]

Brigham Young: "This American continent will be Zion; for it is so spoken of by the prophets. Jerusalem will be rebuilt and will be the new place of gathering, and the tribe of Judah will gather there, but this continent of America is the land of Zion. Zion will extend, eventually, all over this earth. There will be no nook or corner upon the earth but will be in Zion. It will all be Zion."[4]

Recently at a Book of Mormon conference Mr. Meldrum said, "What did Joseph Smith know about Book of Mormon geography?" Answering this question he said:

"The Wentworth letter was published on 1 March, 1842, in the Times and Seasons. Quoting only part, Joseph Smith said, 'On the evening of 21 September, A.D. 1823, while I was praying unto God, ..., In a moment a personage stood before me, surrounded with glory yet greater than that with which I was already surrounded. This messenger proclaimed himself to be an Angel of God... I was also informed concerning the aboriginal inhabitants of this country and was shown who they were, and from whence they came; a brief sketch of their origin, progress, civilization, laws, governments, of their

[3] Ibid pp. 122 – 123
[4] Ibid p. 120

righteousness and iniquity, and the blessings of God being finally withdrawn from them as a people, was made known unto me.'"

David Hyrum Smith's Vision of Hill Cumorah

CHAPTER 24

The youngest of the nine children born to Emma and Joseph Smith Jr., David Hyrum came into the world on 14 November 1844 in the Old Homestead, in Nauvoo, Illinois. Five months before his birth, his father had been killed by a mob in Carthage, Illinois. A fail, colicky baby, he was cherished by his widowed mother, his elder (and adopted) sister, Julia, his brothers, Joseph III, Frederick, and Alexander. He was three years old when his mother married Louis C. Bidamon. With that marriage he gained two step sisters, Mary Elizabeth 11, and Emma Zereida Bidamon, 13, who, like so many other children, were welcome by his mother who could never stand to see a soul in need go without giving aid.[1]

A list of poems were compiled in a book by David titled 'Songs of Endless Life and Other Poems'. It was published

---

[11] 'David Hyrum Smith', by Gracia Jones, 10 Dec. 2004

by Herald Publishing House in 1875 at Lamoni, Iowa. I would like to share one of sixty-four poems at my fingertips. Though David did not know his father in this life, he saw the hill Cumorah upon this land of North America in a vision and the records hidden within. He wrote this experience down and placed in his book of poems.

HILL CUMORAH

*While the years unnoted run their fruitless courses toward the west,
And the world in darkness struggled for the light of truth expressed,
There lay hid on Hill Cumorah's rocky mountain slope, in trust,
Truths that yet should rise and smite the ancient idols into dust;*

*While the older world was troubled with her pestilence and war;
While her soldiers fought for Jesus, or for Jove, or yet for Thor;
While great empires faltered and went down to death and shame,
And their rivals through red carnage fought their way to transient fame.*

*In the deep and somber forests of a newer world there lay
Golden records that were guarded by a greater yet than they.
Hill Cumorah kept his silent watch and counted still the days
When the sun slid down his mighty arch into the evening haze.*

And the angel footsteps pressed his rugged brow and passed away
From their vigils o'er the rough-hewn casket where the records lay;
From their watching and their praying for the time so long deferred,
When the gospel trump again should sound, the gospel truth be heard,

Till the ears of man were ripe to hear, the lips of men to speak;
Till the souls of men were hungry, and the hearts of men were meek;
Till a few should turn from fables, and a few should come to prove
What the learned could never answer and the mighty never move.

Like the fretful waves that circle where swift, mighty currents sweep
Rise the waves of persecution, but they never stir the deep.
Like the little waves that run to meet and break upon the sand,
They can never shake the granite cliffs where Truth and Reason stand.

Be not fearful; we are working with the Infinite and Just
Who has caused the truth to spring from earth, the gospel from the dust.
We it is who have the message and the precious truths of old.
Angels guard us as they guarded where were hid the plates of gold.

Let the soul that hears the message haste to spread the world abroad.
Let him hold the record closely, and be faithful unto God,
Faithful as the Hill Cumorah; though no man shall see his strength,

*God shall find the heart where truth is hid, and
bring it forth at length.*

David's book provided a small income for his wife, Clara
Hartsshom Smith and son Elbert. David crossed over on
29 August 1904 a few months short of his sixtieth
birthday.

Heavenly Beings Watch Over Us

CHAPTER 25

No individual after reading the Book of Mormon, having the spirit of the Lord as his guide, then onto his knees praying for confirmation by the power of the Holy Ghost can stand up not knowing within the depths of his soul that it came from God.[1]

About 34 A.D. in the ancient land of Bountiful, south of the Great Lakes in the Ohio River valley, the people had gathered around the temple.[2] A voice quietly speaks. Again the voice speaks. 'And again the third time they did hear the voice, and did open their ears to hear it; and their eyes were towards the sound thereof; and they did look steadfastly towards heaven, from whence the sound came.' And the voice said, 'Behold my "Beloved Son, in

---

[1] Moroni 10:4-5
[2] 'The Book of Mormon in America's Heartland', by Rod L. Meldrum, June 2011, p. 199, www.BookOfMormonEvidence.org.

whom I am well pleased, in whom I have glorified my name - - hear ye him"".[3]

Can you imagine what it would have been like to be a fly on the wall taking it all in? What a glorious event. "They cast their eyes up again toward heaven; and behold, they saw a man descending out of heaven; and he was clothed in a white robe; and he came down and stood in the midst of them; and the eyes of the whole multitude were turned upon him, and they durst not speak even to one another."[4]

Amongst this people Jesus chose twelve disciples and organized His church. Three of the twelve wanted to linger until the Second Coming with power over death. They wanted to center their lives on charity, helping others come unto Christ. Nine of twelve disciples desired and are promised an inheritance in Christ's kingdom when they die.[5]

The ancient prophet Mormon recorded: "Whether they are mortal or immortal, from the day of their transfiguration, I know not." Then after praying and pondering about their status, he said, "Since I wrote, I have inquired of the Lord, and he hath made it manifest unto me that there must needs be a change wrought upon their bodies or else it needs be that they must taste of death; therefore, that they might not taste of death there was a change wrought upon their bodies, that they might not suffer pain or sorrow save it were for the sins of the world."[6]

---

[3] 3 Nephi 11:7
[4] 3 Nephi 11:5
[5] Book of Mormon, 3 Nephi 28
[6] Book of Mormon, 3 Nephi 28:37-39 also Mormon 8:10-11

Moroni added his testimony, "But behold, my father and I have seen them, and they have ministered unto us."[7]

A change was wrought upon the Three Nephites insomuch that Satan hath no power over them. Even in our time Satan hath no power over them. There is no power in the earth that can hold them, contain them, or direct their actions. Each are free to interact with the people who need help spiritually, physically (sickness) or temporally. Their main objective is in bringing people unto Christ and charity is the center of their thoughts. Translated beings have the power to appear out of nowhere and also instantly vanish from sight.

James E. Talmage stated, "Because of God's great love, he has sent heavenly beings to watch over us and to guard us from the attack of evil powers while we live on earth. Do we realize that in our daily walk and work we are not alone, but that angels attend us wherever our duty causes us to go?"[8]

Lucy Mack Smith stated that her son Joseph was so familiar with "the ancient inhabitants of this continent" that he could describe their customs, clothing, cities and practices of worship. Could it be possible that the Three Nephites visited at times with the prophet and gave him a grand tour of the heartland of America by vision or otherwise? Lucy stated that Joseph "would describe the ancient inhabitants as to the dress, mode of travel, and the animals upon which they rode; their cities, their building with every particular; their tools of warfare; also their way of worship and religion. This Joseph would do

---

[7] Book of Mormon, 3 Nephi 28:25-27
[8] 'Millennial Star 55', July 10, 1893, p. 446; also Collected Discourses 3:291.

with as much ease, as if he had spent his entire life with them".[9]

In our day, Boyd K. Packer declared, "The promptings of the Spirit, the dreams, and the visions, and the visitations, and the ministering of angels all are with us now."[10]

---

[9] 'Letter by Helen Mar Whitney tells of a visit of a Nephite to Joseph Smith'; see 'Holzapfal, Woman's View', p. 173. Also "Parting of the Veil", in Welch and Carlson, 'Opening the Heavens', p. 271.
[10] 'Revelations in a Changing World', Ensign, Nov. 1989, p. 16.

No Mercy for the Pequot's

CHAPTER 26

Brigham Young spoke regarding murder, "I spoke a harsh word yesterday with regard to a man who professes to be a Latter-day Saint who has been guilty of killing an innocent Indian. I say today that he is just as much a murderer through killing that Indian, as he would have been had he shot down a white man. To slay an innocent person is murder according to the law of Moses."[1]

"Do we wish to do right? You answer, yes. Then let the Lamanites come back to their homes, where they were born and brought up. This is the land that they and their fathers have walked over and called their own; and they have just as good a right to call it theirs today as any people have to call any land their own. They have buried their fathers and mothers and children here; this is their

---

[1] 'Journal of Discourses' 11:263

home, and we have taken possession of it; and occupy the land . . ."[2]

In 1636 a British Army is about to ravage upon the Pequot Indians who were living on Block Island. This planned attack is under the command of Endicott which greatly upset the chief of the Pequot tribe living upon the mainland. The chief demanded a surrender of those soldiers whom performed the deadly deed of murder upon his people and pointed out the English had broken many promises.[3]

English soldiers attacked the Pequot Indians on the eastern mainland killing many, seizing their corn, burning their crops, spoiling what they could not carry away. War was now upon them, the white man living in Connecticut wanted their land. Many Indians already died from the white man's disease of small pox and the common cold. Thousands died with graves unknown.[4]

During the winter of 1636-37 the Pequot tribe was lacking food so they attacked several small farm communities. The news went out that the savages were on the war path killing and horribly mutilating the bodies. There was no mention of the murders committed upon the Pequot so the English thought they had an excuse to kill them - mass murder.

Spirits were running high among the settlers, they sought help from Boston and Plymouth. The British sent out

[2] 'Journal of Discourses' 11:264, Also 'Discourses of Brigham Young' by John A. Widtsoe, 1966 edition, Deseret Book Company, pp. 122-123. Also Book of Mormon, 4 Nephi 1:1-45 and 3 Nephi 11:4-15
[3] 'The Pilgrim Fathers of New England', by John Brown, B.A., D.D.; 3rd Edition, printed 1906, pp. 306-307
[4] Ibid. p. 307

ninety soldiers heavily armed under the command of John Mason. Under his direction a plan was devised to kill the entire Pequot tribe. The original tribe was over thirty thousand, now dwindled down to less than eight hundred.[5] On a moonlight night in May 1637, Commander John Mason planned a surprise attack. There would be no mercy upon the Pequot people.

As a last stand the Indians set up in their stronghold; one designed for protection for their wives, children, grandparents, etc. Just like in the Book of Mormon days, an entrenched fort, a walled village, girted by an earthen rampart three feet high and a palisade twelve feet high made of sturdy saplings set firm and deep into the ground. At the opposite ends were two openings barely large enough to let a man pass through, and within this enclosure of three acres were the crowded wigwams of families.

A little before daybreak both entrances were occupied by Commander Mason's soldiers and the entrenchment was taken by complete surprise. Seized with panic, the Pequots tried to escape through first one outlet and then the other but were ruthlessly shot down whichever way they turned.

The British soldiers shot firebrands over the tall palisade among the wigwams; soon the whole place was in flames, the Indians perishing in their burning dwellings. Seven hundred Pequots – men, women, children of all ages died with no mercy from the English. Only five Pequots

---

[5] Ibid. p. 307

escaped with their lives. The English had only sixteen slightly wounded soldiers and two were killed.[6]

Never had the Indians heard of so terrible a vengeance. The Indians did not lift their hands against the white man until thirty-eight years later at the time of King Philips War.[7]

Why did this have to happen? It opened up the land for the white man. The Connecticut settlements were no longer isolated and it consolidated New England.

[6] Ibid., p. 308
[7] Ibid., p. 308

CHAPTER 27

In 1620 Massachusetts was settled as a colony. Its greatest cause of anxiety for the first century of its growth was from war with the Native Americans. One peacemaker, an Indian Chief, 'Massasoit' kept faith with the white men; however after his death his son 'Metacomet' whom the white men called Philip became chief of his community. King Philip was a brave warrior, a man of superior mind and was not contented with the rapid inroads which the English were making in a land which had once belonged to the Lamanite nation. "The white man kept crowding us farther and farther from the places we had called our own."

King Metacomet (Philip) called for an act of war and shortly made a treaty with one of the neighboring tribes – the Narragansett's. The two large Tribes united making great havoc up and down the Connecticut River valley oft' times attacking churches. Soon massacre and fighting were everywhere. Sometimes a party of white men fell upon a party of red men in their wigwams and slew them all – warriors, old men, and even children.

The war became evil. The white man soldiers had taken the body of an Indian woman, a princess of her tribe, who tried hard to escape by swimming the river and was drowned. They were not content with finding her body but cut her head off with a sword then paraded it around on a pole.

King Philip's War with the English heightened in the summer of 1675 and on into the winter with much suffering on both sides. The towns of Brookfield and Deerfield were burnt to the ground. A terrible battle was fought near Deerfield, which was later referred to as the "Battle of Bloody Brook". Connecticut had kept clear of the war, Rhode Island had kept peace but Massachusetts (colony of my relatives from my dad's mother's side) had suffered terribly. Many of my relatives died in this war. The state of Massachusetts lost one man out of every twenty, and one family out of each twenty had lost their homes.

The stories above and below were written into our U.S. History Book by Abby Sage Richardson, published by The Riverside Press, Cambridge, 1880, pp. 131-132. The book sat many years at the Sherburn Merrill Smith Memorial Public Library in Wendell, Idaho and is now a favorite history book in my home library.

My grandmother, Edith Adams Smith, shared in our family history book the same story as Abby:

"It was during the 'King Philip's War' an incident which I'm about to share occurred. It was shortly after June 1675. A family member, Thomas Eames, had rented a farm and built a house on the southern slope of Mt. Wayte, between Sudbury River and farm pond; seven miles southwest of the town of Sudbury. Later it became Framingham, just three miles east of the Indian town of Magunook.

"The greater part of the Christian Indians had disarmed trusting in our government, and were sent to Deer Island; where according to Chief Gookin they suffered extreme hardships. Netus an Indian Chief of a small band of bad Indians lived a short distance from Thomas Eames' log house and farm. The Eames family consisted of Thomas, his wife Mary, her six children, and Margaret a daughter of his first wife.

"While Thomas was away to Boston for a supply of ammunition about a dozen Indians led by Netus attacked the family. Mary Eames was making soap and poured upon the assailants the boiling fluid. All the family were either killed or captured. The house, barn and all the belongings were burned to the ground even the animals, hay, and grain in the barn.

"Out of the family of ten, only three were returned, Samuel, Nathaniel and Margaret. Joseph Adams was among those sent to obtain their release, fell in love with Margaret, and married her in 1688."

Grandmother Smith also mentioned another attack upon my family members in and around the town of Hadley, Massachusetts.

"Many had gathered on a Sunday morning in a small log cabin church to worship their God. All the old men and young men, mothers with nursing babies in their arms, maidens and little children were in the house of worship. The minister was at prayer, with the whole congregation still as death. Suddenly arose the wild cry, 'The Indians! The Indians!'

"Every man seized the gun which stood by him. The women huddled the children together and stood close in the little log church, with faces pale as death. The men met the red foe bravely, but the surprise was so great, and the numbers so unequal, that the warring Indians were fast gaining an advantage.

"All at once in the middle of the battle *appeared a man of towering height, with long streaming hair, beard, and dressed in a wild fashion.* He suddenly appeared among the white men like a strong deliverer. Where ever the towering stranger went the Indians fell before him. The courage of the English church goers began to rise . . . The man saved the lives of their families. When the fight ended without a word the towering stranger disappeared as quickly as he had come. It was almost like he was a 'translated warrior' from another world or time period. Many believed to their dying day he was not a mortal man."

A Stranger at Massacre Point

CHAPTER 28

One September not too long ago, as the leaves start turning amber and with early morning sunshine I knew it was time to go fishing. It has not been a good year for fishing, I've been out ten times on the Snake River, always at a favorite spot; yet for some reason I'm not connecting with the bass or rainbow trout. I don't understand why the fish are not biting. Not even a trash fish has crossed my hook. There is a lot on my mind. Last January I finished forty-three chapters of a second book then decided not to print it so the rough copies are just in stacks collecting dust in my home office. My first book, Keeper of the Prophet's Sword was not about me. This book is different.

I quickly load my fishing gear into my Toyota Corolla, pack a few snacks, put ice in the cooler, add cookies to the list and point the car toward Massacre Point. Before I realize it I am there. This is my favorite spot, its mid-week and no one is around.

I'm fishing at a different spot, a place on top of a fishing ramp, a spot not designated for boats just a place to hang out on a floating ramp. It's a time to be lazy, soak up the sun drink a cola and an occasional sip of water. There are roasted peanuts, a cookie or two, salted chips and a sandwich for later. It's a bit of heaven on the floating ramp - my spot tucked away on the Snake River. It's just me and the ducks.

Yes! This is my day, I will not return home empty-handed. It's time to break the no fish spell. There is no excuse to leave empty handed, it is in the middle of the week after Labor Day. But I'm down in spirits just wanting to be by myself and think things through. As a protector of Joseph Smith's 'Legion Sword' Satan has singled me out making several attempts to take my life. There have been lightning strikes, a truck flying down upon me off a freeway ramp, a bullet whizzing by my ear, and many other events on the road or at home.

Suddenly out of nowhere there is a crushing of rolling rocks on my backside. I think, great here we go a family is sliding down the rocky cliff to take my favorite fishing spot. Looking over my shoulder I'm greatly surprised, it's a man sliding down the cliff with a fishing rod in hand and making a commotion of rolling rocks. Why is he doing this? There is a pathway that is quite obvious, 30 feet from his left side, leading to my fishing ramp. My fishing ramp, my spot!

I experienced an attitude change almost instantly as his presence sent the Holy Ghost upon me. As I stand up he said, "Hi, how's the fishing?" I responded, "Very slow today." He had a glow about him, and he said, "If you don't mind can I fish on that rock just upstream a little bit from you?" He was different yet I can't put my finger on it. He had a white glow about his body, he was very friendly with a wide smile crossing his face. I felt something like I've never felt before. It's quite difficult to write down on paper or to share.

The friendly stranger said, "A mep spinner would be great up against the overhanging cliff just below you, surely you'll catch something there." I said, "Have you fished here before? Where's your home?" With a smile he said, "I'm from the Mississippi valley - it is my homeland."

The stranger looked to be in his late forty's, around five feet ten inches tall, one hundred seventy pounds or so, light skin (lacking a tan), strawberry gray hair below the shoulders neatly trimmed and tied into a ponytail. He wore a wide brim hat, summer shorts just below the knee, a long sleeve shirt which was untucked, and he sports a strawberry colored beard neatly trimmed with streaks of gray. I noticed he was very light on his feet.

As I look in his direction I see that he is not prepared for fishing. He has no krill, no net, no tackle box, nothing to drink, no lunch, and his spinning rod looks very outdated. I said, "My friend, cast up and out into the headwaters, I've caught many trout in that spot." He said, "Thanks for sharing your fishing spot. All I have to fish with is my old spinning rod, a line tied to a rusty piece of iron with a triple hook." I thought that was funny, he must be kidding. No one in his right mind would be fishing the Snake River with a rusty homemade lure.

Who is the stranger, from whence did he come? I looked cross-eyed as he made his way over the rocks and willows then perched upon a large lava rock. He was within talking distance and he was so friendly that he became my new fishing buddy. He stood straight as an arrow, making a cast with his old spinning rod very precisely into the upper portion of the river. He did not get into my space, he honored the rules of fishing.

Almost instantly this man is my friend. He seems exceptionally smart, angelic like, different, and the kind of person that rarely crosses ones path. I will share all my fishing secrets with him.

But first a brief history of Massacre Point . . . I then explained to him the Idaho state fishing rules, the need for a fishing license, the two pole rule, entry fees at the gate, catch and release for bass under twelve inches, two bass creel limit, and the six trout rule. Smiling at me he said, "An entry fee, size limit, fishing license. It makes no sense. I don't have a license." I said, "Have you fished earlier today?" He said, "No, I left California this morning." I asked him if he had family there. He said, "No, someone there needed my help and I was there to assist." When he said that I thought it was strange. It's just a little past noon, with over a twelve hour drive to here. It made no sense.

Several casts were made by my new friend, each flying over and above the river with precision, landing his spoon into the headwater just above my fishing hole. I'm sitting on the dock with my pole in hand also making several casts with my shiny bright spinner. To be honest, I was attempting to impress the stranger with my acquired fishing skills; yet I was in complete wonderment as to his precision with every cast, his lure went out way beyond mine. In silence he turned to smile in my direction.

Suddenly I look up with amazement. My new friend has hooked a very large fish near the middle of the river. His ancient pole was severely bent, his face kept looking my way as if to say I need your help. I said to him, "You need a net. I'll be right there". I grab my long handled net and immediately sprang into action I feared the worst that the fish may break the line or spit the hook out. The pole is bending more and more as I make my way across the sharp lava rock, hugging the brush, and clinging onto the willows. I make my way to his side, his fishing pole is bent and the head of a trophy rainbow trout partially out of the water. He looks up with a smile as if to say what do I do now?

I'm standing on the edge of a large lava rock viewing a huge rainbow trout just below my feet and there to assist my friend. Yet I'm not in a position to reach the fish with my hand net so I quickly hand the net to him. With his fishing pole in his left hand and the line straight as an arrow, he manages to grab the five foot handle net and, to my amazement, scoops the open net across the head of the trout over and over again each time looking my way with panic in his eyes as if to say 'What should I do to land this trophy fish?'. The net cannot go over the head of the trout, the line is straight extending from the tip of the fishing pole to the hook in the lip of the fish.

Sensing that my new friend is 'toying' with me it is yet a teaching moment. The fishing spoon barely hooked into the fish's mouth is just an old piece of rusty iron with a large triple hook. Quickly I said, "Take the open net over the tail of the fish then scoop it up and out of the water." Scooping the fish into the net it stays contained in the bindings of the net. It is quite a catch.

I said to him, "Let's get your fish onto a stringer." He said, "I don't have a stringer so this trout is yours for being so nice to me." "No, you can't do that it's your fish. You caught it." "No, it's your fish. I want you to have it, you're my friend." "Are you sure?" "Yes." "Thank you very much." With the fish net in my hand we shake hands as a bond of friendship and with tears in my eyes I thanked him again for the fish. I received a heavy dose of the Holy Ghost at that moment and was humbled in the presence of this man from the Mississippi valley area.

I invited him to join me on the ramp and we made our way there quickly. I said, "Let's do some more fishing." He said, "No I need to be on my way." I asked him where he was headed. He said, "I need to be in Billings, Montana by early afternoon to help someone in need. After that I'm on my way back home for supper."

Extending my hand I introduce myself. He extended his hand saying his name; it's a long word starting with a 'K'. He had no last name. The name passed through my mind quickly so I asked his name again, and again and it quickly left my mind. Perhaps the third time would be the charm, but no such luck. We put the fish on my stringer. The fish weighing close to ten pounds.

Standing on the fishing ramp – eyes to eyes – hand in hand – the stranger looked into my soul. Teary eyed I stated "Hopefully someday I'll cross your path in heaven above." Placing his hand on my shoulder he said, "Howard, how do you know that? Maybe I will go into hell." With a smile on his face he pointed a finger down into the river. I said, with a smile, "I just know. You are my friend." He goes up the rocky cliff with pole in hand and disappears.

After my friend leaves I ponder this happen-stance experience. It just didn't make any sense. How could this man possibly be in California early in the morning, at Massacre Point, Idaho at noon, in the mid-afternoon be in Billings, Montana, and then back to the Mississippi valley for dinner tonight. It suddenly occurs to me that he is a translated being. A man from the Book of Mormon days. An angel who likes to fish. This is awesome! Why me? No one but my wife will believe me.

Translated beings are described thus, "They are as the Angels of God, and if they shall pray unto the Father in the name of Jesus they can show themselves unto whatsoever man it seemeth them good. Therefore great and marvelous works shall be wrought by them, before the great and coming day when all people must surely stand before the judgment seat of Christ; yea even among the Gentiles shall there be a great and marvelous work wrought by them before the judgment day.[1]

Around 32 A.D. the prophet Mormon wrote the names of the twelve disciples called by Jesus. "And it came to pass that on the morrow, when the multitude was gathered together, behold, Nephi and his brother whom he had raised from the dead, whose name was Timothy, and also his son, whose name was Jonas, and also Mathoni, and Mathonihah, his brother, and Kumen, and Kumenonhi, and Jeremiah, and Shemnon, and Jonas, and Zedekiah, and Isaiah - now these were the names of the disciples whom Jesus had chosen - and it came to pass that they went forth and stood in the midst of the multitude.[2]

---

[1] Book of Mormon, 3 Nephi 28:27 – 32
[2] Book of Mormon, 3 Nephi 19:3-4

Zedekiah, Kumenonhi, Jeremiah, when those three apostles "were caught up into heaven", what happened to them? Franklin D. Richards's comments: "They wanted to tarry until Jesus came, and that they might, he took them into the heavens and endowed them with the power of translation, probably in one of Enoch's temples, and brought them back to earth. Thus they received power to live until the coming of the Son of Man. I believe he took them to Enoch's city and gave them their endowments there."[3]

There is much more to the story, but I end it here.

---

[3] Elder Franklin D Richards, talk given at Tabernacle, May 17, 1844, recorded in the 'Journal of Discourses', Vol. 25, pp. 236 – 237.

In Our Day — Enoch & His Holy City

CHAPTER 29

Enoch and his holy city live in our day beyond our earth in outer space, on a chunk of earth that left our planet and attached itself onto a terrestrial planet. Someday, years ahead, Enoch and his people will return to mother earth and the chunk of earth will reattach itself from whence it left.

At this time Enoch and the people within his city live without discord or dissention; they are angelic, translated beings, wise and gentle, without malice or deceit, constantly visiting each other. They are incorruptible and hence without death; they do not grow old or wear out; their nature is unfailing. There are magnificent buildings which stand beside tranquil seas and flowing springs which give life-giving water. Everything vibrates with joy. The wants of the people are few. They move through the air by an effortless power of flight; they are home in the firmaments and the worlds and among all the dominions and powers.[1]

There is a perfect agreement among the worlds, each having its particular glory and rejoicing in the glory of the others as all share their treasures of knowledge. They are vast distances removed from each other, but through their common Lord and God they share a common glorious awareness of each other. Each of these worlds is a Zion, having no law courts, no hunger or thirst, no cold or heat, no hatred or fear, no war, no slavery, no harmful creatures or plants.[2]

"And the Lord said unto Enoch; As I live, even so will I come in the last days, in the days of wickedness and vengeance, to fulfill the oath which I have made unto you concerning the children of Noah;[3]

"And it came to pass that Enoch saw the day of the coming of the Son of Man in the last days, to dwell on the earth in righteousness for the space of a thousand years;[4]

". . . and righteousness and truth will I cause to sweep the earth as with a flood, to gather out mine elect from the four quarters of the earth, unto a place which I shall prepare, an Holy City, that my people may gird up their loins, and be looking forth for the time of my coming, for there shall be my Tabernacle, and it shall be called Zion, a New Jerusalem."[5]

---

[1] 'A Strange Thing in the Lord: The Return of the Book of Enoch, Part 12', by Hugh Nibley, June 1977, p. 383
[2] Ibid, p. 383
[3] Pearl of Great Price, Moses 7:60
[4] Pearl of Great Price, Moses 7:65
[5] Pearl of Great Price, Moses 7:62

Into the millennium a wonderful reunion will take place between the people of Enoch and the Saints who will be upon the earth at this time. The Lord declared to Enoch, "Then shalt thou and all thy city meet them there, and we will receive them into our bosom, and they shall see us; and we will fall upon their necks and they shall fall upon ours and we will kiss each other."[6]

What a wonderful event it will be to attend. Where will this take place? Zion, home of the Saints. Independence, Jackson County, Missouri will be the center stake of Zion in the City of Zion also known as "The New Jerusalem". This temple site was dedicated August 3, 1821.[7] The City of Zion will be after the order of the 'City of Enoch'. There will be three capital cities; namely 'Zion or the New Jerusalem'; Jerusalem, as we know it today, the gathering place of the Jews; and the City of Enoch.

---

[6] Moses 7:63
[7] 'Essentials in Church History' page 134

A New Ridge of Land to Appear

CHAPTER 30

The coming of the Ten Tribes from the north countries will not be an ordinary event. For hundreds of years their prophets have been preparing. In 1831 the Lord revealed to his prophet Joseph Smith that the translated apostle John was fulfilling a mission among the Ten Tribes preparing them for their journey to Zion.[1]

When the Lord commands it, and the earth has been prepared for it, the prophets who are living among them will "no longer stay themselves but will bring forth their multitudes."[2]

Where are these translated people? Joseph Fielding Smith in his book The Way to Perfection maintains "They are not a scattered people, but are a separate body and will

[1] Smith, 'Essentials in Church History', p. 126
[2] D&C 133:26

return in a group."[3] Could it possibly be that the more righteous were translated and taken up?

Where are they? An answer may well be found with a song written by Eliza R. Snow titled 'Where are the Lost Tribes?'

1. *Thou, earth, was once a glorious sphere*
   Of noble magnitude,
   And didst with majesty appear
   Among the worlds of God

2. *But thy dimensions have been torn*
   Asunder, piece by piece
   And each dissembled fragment borne
   Abroad to distant space

3. *When Enoch could no longer stay*
   Amid corruption here,
   Part of thyself was borne away
   To form another sphere.

4. *That portion where his city stood*
   He gained by right approved;
   And nearer to the throne of God
   His planet upward moved

5. *And when the Lord saw fit to hide*
   The "ten lost tribes" away,
   Thou earth was severed to provide
   The orb on which they stay

6. *And thus, from time to time, thy size*
   Has been diminished 'til
   Thou seem'st the law of sacrifice
   Created to fulfill.[4]

---

[3] 'The Way to Perfection', by Joseph Fielding Smith, 6th Edition, 1946, p. 337
[4] Hymns, 322 (C.M.)

In the early 1830's Joseph Smith was visiting with Benjamin Brown and his family. Benjamin shared his story with his grandson, Homer M. Brown, who later became a Patriarch of the Granite Stake (Utah). At that time Homer shared an interview:

"Brother Brown, will you give us some light and explanation of the 5th verse on page 286 of the Hymn book which speaks of the ten tribes of Israel, or the part of this earth which formed another planet, according to the Hymn of Eliza R. Snow."

"Yes, sir. I think I can answer your question. Sister Eliza R. Snow, in visiting my grandparents, was asked by my grandmother: 'Eliza, where did you get your ideas about the ten lost tribes being taken away as you explained it in your wonderful hymn?' She answered as follows: 'Why, my husband told me about it.'"

"Have you any other information that your grandfather ever gave you, as contained in any conversation with the prophet Joseph Smith?" "I have! One evening in Nauvoo, just after dark, somebody rapped at the door very vigorously. Grandfather said he was reading the Doctrine and Covenants. He rose hurriedly and answered the summons at the door, where he met the prophet Joseph Smith."

"He said, 'Brother Brown, can you keep me over night, the mobs are after me?' Grandfather answered, 'Yes, sir. It will not be the first time, come in.' 'All right,' the prophet said, shutting the door quickly. He came in and sat down. Grandmother said, 'Brother Joseph, have you had your supper?' 'No', he answered, 'I have not.' So she prepared him a meal and he ate it.

Afterward they were in conversation relative to the principles of the Gospel. During the conversation the ten lost tribes were mentioned. Grandfather said, 'Joseph, where are the ten tribes?' He said, 'Come to the door and I will show you, come on sister Brown, I want you both to see.'

"It being a starlight night the prophet said: 'Brother Brown, can you show me the Polar Star?' 'Yes, sir.' He said, pointing to the North Star. 'There it is.' 'Yes, I know,' said the prophet, 'but which one? There are a lot of stars there.' Grandfather said, 'Can you see the points of the Dipper?' The prophet answered, 'Yes.' 'Well' he said, 'trace the pointers,' pointing up on to the largest star. 'That is the North Star."

"The prophet answered: 'You are correct. 'Now,' he said, pointing toward the star, 'do you discern a little twinkle to the right and below the Polar Star, which we would judge to be about the distance of 20 feet from here?' Grandfather answered, 'Yes, sir.' The prophet said: 'Sister Brown, do you see that star also?' Her answer was, 'Yes, sir.' 'Very well then, he said, 'Let's go in.'

"After re-entering the house, the prophet said: 'Brother Brown, I noticed when I came in that you were reading the Doctrine and Covenants. Will you kindly get it?' He did so. The prophet turned to Section 133 and read, commencing at the 26th verse and throughout to the 34th verse."

"And they who are in the north countries shall come in remembrance before the Lord; and their prophets shall hear His voice, and shall no longer stay themselves; and

they shall smite the rocks, and the ice shall flow down at their presence.

And an highway shall be cast up in the midst of the great deep.

Their enemies shall become a prey unto them.

And in the barren deserts there shall come forth pools of living water; and the parched ground shall no longer be a thirsty land.

And they shall bring forth their rich treasures unto the children of Ephraim, my servants.

And the boundaries of the everlasting hills shall tremble at their presence.

And there shall they fall down and be crowned with glory, even in Zion, by the hands of the servants of the Lord, even the children of Ephraim.

And they shall be filled with songs of everlasting joy."

"He said, after reading the 31st verse, 'Now let me ask you what would cause the everlasting hills to tremble with more violence than the coming together of the two planets? And the place whereon they reside will return to this earth. Now,' he said, 'Scientists will tell you that it is not scientific; that two planets coming together would be disastrous to both; but, when two planets or other objects are traveling in the same direction and one of them with a little greater velocity than the other, it would not be disastrous, because the one traveling faster would overtake the other. Now, what would cause the mountains of ice to melt quicker than the heat caused by the friction of the two planets coming together?' And then he asked the question, 'Did you ever see a meteor falling that was not red hot? So what would cause the mountains of ice to melt?'

"'And relative to the great highway which should be cast up when the planet returns to its place in the great northern waters, it will form a highway and waters will recede and roll back.' He continued, 'Now as to their coming back from the northern waters; they will return from the north because their planet will return to the place from whence it was taken. Relative to the waters rolling back to the north. If you take a vessel of water and swing it rapidly around your head you won't spill any, but if you stop the motion gradually, it will begin to pour out. Now,' he said, 'Brother Brown, at the present time this earth is rotating very rapidly. When this planet returns it will make the earth that much heavier, and it will then revolve slower, and that will account for the waters receding from the earth for a great while, but it has now turned and is proceeding rapidly eastward.'"[5]

When the piece of earth returns with the righteous people the equilibrium of the center of the earth will become altered and great earthquakes will be felt around the world. Extinct volcanoes will become active, tidal waves and cyclones will cause enormous destruction.[6]

An earthquake will develop northeasterly starting in the Pacific coast of Peru, passing through Panama, Mexico, United States, and Canada and into the Arctic regions. New York, Washington, Boston, other eastern cities, and

---

[5] 'The Last Days', Compiled by Robert W. Smith, Oct. 1931, 6th Edition, July, 1943, pp. 217-220
[6] 'Cherio's Prediction', Deseret News, 1934

Toronto will be seriously affected and a considerable part of New York will be destroyed.[7]

Mountains, ice, and a continent of water will stand between the Ten Tribes and the land of Zion when they first appear. They will smite the rocks, and the ice shall flow down at their presence.[8] Could this be "global warming" that some "experts" talk about? As the Ten Tribes come to the great body of water, dry land will be cast up in the mist of it so that a mighty highway will spread before them. The ocean between Alaska, USA and Russia is very shallow. Could it be that this is part of the dry land that will be cast up?

Their enemies shall become a prey unto them.[9] Those who once sought to conquer or injure the ten tribes will instead be subject to them. In other words, no enemy will be able to permanently hinder the progress of Israel as she returns to God and to those promises which the Lord has made to her.

Where will the hosts of Israel dwell? When they return, Joseph Smith predicted, if the gentile civilization now inhabiting this land (America) should become unworthy of it; the Lord Jesus Christ has warned that he will rid this land of any unworthy people. He said, "There would be ample room for the hosts of Israel when they do come."[10]

"The Temple in Jackson County will be built in this generation. The saints will think there will not be time to build it, but with all the help you will receive you can put

---

[7] Ibid

[8] D&C 133:26

[9] D&C 133:28

[10] Smith, ;Teachings of the Prophet Joseph Smith', p. 17

up a great temple quickly. They will have all the gold, silver, and precious stones; for these things only will be used for the beautifying of the temple; all the skilled mechanics you want, and the Ten Tribes of Israel will help you build it. When you see this land bound with iron you may look toward Jackson County.[11] Could the words, "this land bound with iron" mean a loss of freedom and individual rights for the citizens of the United States of America?

Their return will be a glorious event; they will open up their records, histories, genealogy of families, and scriptures sharing all with the saints.[12] It shall come down in a day, when 'your old men shall have dreams, your young men shall see visions.[13] Alas for the day! For the day of the Lord is at hand, and as a destruction from the Almighty shall it come.[14]

The American Prophet, Joseph Smith, speaks out into our day: "And now I am prepared to say by the authority of Jesus Christ that not many years shall pass away before the United States shall present such a scene of bloodshed as has not been paralleled in the history of our nation; pestilence, hail, famine, and earthquake will sweep the wicked of this generation from off the face of the land, to open and prepare the way for the return of the Lost Ten Tribes of Israel from the north country."[15]

---

[11] 'Prophet Joseph Smith – uttered in the presence of Edwin Rushton and Theodore Turley, on or about May 6, 1843'.
[12] Book of Mormon 2 Nephi 29:12-13
[13] Old Testament, Joel 2:28
[14] Old Testament, Joel 1:15
[15] 'Excerpts from a sermon of the Prophet Joseph Smith', Vol. I, Church History, Jan 4, 1883, p. 315. Also 'The Last Days', 6th Edition, by Smith, 1943, p. 37.

Death shall be Sweet unto Them

CHAPTER 31

"He that liveth when the Lord shall come, and hath kept the faith, blessed is he; nevertheless, it is appointed to him to die at the age of man. Wherefore, children shall grow up until they become old; old men shall die; but they shall not sleep in the dust, but they shall be changed in the twinkling of an eye."[1] What a blessing to go from this mortality to immortality almost instantaneously!

But the Lord says of all his saints, not that they will not die, but that "those that die in me shall not taste of death, for it shall be sweet unto them; and they that die not in me, wo unto them, for their death is bitter."[2]

"Death hath passed upon all men, to fulfil the merciful plan of the great Creator."[3] There are no exceptions, not even among translated people such as Enoch's people. This includes families of husbands, wives and children.

---

[1] D & C 63:50-51
[2] D & C 42:46-47
[3] 2 Nephi 9:6

Paul said: "As in Adam all die, even so in Christ shall all be made alive."[4]

Translated people do not suffer physical death as we would normally define it; meaning the separation of body and spirit; nor do they receive a resurrection as we ordinarily describe it, meaning that the body rises from the dust with the spirit entering a renewed perfect home.

The apostle John recorded regarding his own translation: "Then went this saying abroad among the brethren, that the disciple shall not die: yet Jesus said unto him, He shall not die, If I will that he tarry till I come, what is that to thee?"[5]

And even in this state they are to remain until the judgment day of Christ; and in this day they are to receive a greater change soon at hand, and to be received into the kingdom of the Father to go no more out, but to dwell with God eternally in the heavens.

At the Second Coming translated and sanctified beings shall not suffer death as we normally define it. They shall be changed in a twinkling of an eye, and shall be caught up unto a fullness of glory. Death shall be sweet unto them.[6]

---

[4] 1 Cor. 15:22
[5] John 21:23
[6] D & C 101:29-31

A

B

C

D

E

F

G

H

About the Author

Howard Carlos Smith is a native of West Bountiful, Utah and is a research historian in his family. He is the author  of *Keeper of the Prophet's Sword* and *Joseph Smith's Sword And In That Day Miracles & Warnings*. He holds a BS Degree in Automotive Engineering from Utah State University and a Master's Degree in Industrial Education from Brigham Young University. Many years have been spent as an industrial trainer and secondary education teacher. Over 15,000 students have attended his classes.

He has served in various church positions. One of the highlights of his life was serving a two year mission throughout Florida and Puerto Rico for the Church of Jesus Christ of Latter-day Saints. He was one of three missionaries to open up the island of Puerto Rico for the preaching of the Gospel. He has many stories to share on this topic.

He and his wife Jolene share seven children and eight grandchildren. They reside in Burley, Idaho just a few miles from the mighty Snake River and a bit of a distance from Massacre Point.